Exploring the New Role of the Clinical Mental Health Counselor: Vignettes for Best Practices in the Community

BYRD & KERNS

This is a work of fiction. Names, characters, businesses, places, events, locales, and incidents are either the products of the author's imagination or used in a fictitious manner. Any resemblance to actual persons, living or dead, or actual events is purely coincidental.

Copyright © 2018 M. Byrd & K. Kerns

All rights reserved.

ISBN: 0999475827

ISBN-13: 9780999475829

DEDICATION

This book is dedicated to the Clinical Mental Health Counselors making a difference and opening the doors of change….

CONTENTS

Acknowledgments

Section 1

About Authors   7

Purpose   9

Key Terms   10

Introduction   11

Basic Moral Principles   13

Section 2

Vignettes 1-25   17

Section 3

Create Your Own Vignette Instructions   68

Create Your Own Vignette Templates   69

Section 4

Appendix

ACA Ethical Dilemma Process   81

2014 ACA Ethical Standards   82

References   112

ACKNOWLEDGMENTS

We wish to extend special thanks to Trey, Lynelle, Dr. Curtis J. Blakely, Clarissa Singletary, Carrie Purdie, Jacqueline, colleagues, friends, and dear family members.

SECTION 1

ABOUT THE AUTHORS

Melendez O. Byrd, Ph.D.

Dr. Byrd is an Associate Professor at Norfolk State University since 2002, has spent the majority of his career working in the educational arena, specifically in Education, School Counseling, Collegiate Academics, Athletics, Academic Advising and Minority Advancement, which supports the productivity of various types of students. He is committed to teaching, listening, growing, service, scholarship, and research.

His primary objective is to use his educational background expertise and experiences to maximize his impact on education. His goal is to provide accurate academic professional and personal support to *all* students for improving the overall quality of graduate students. Dr. Byrd believes that it is important that counselor educators help develop students' conceptual thinking skills and nurture their inquiring minds regarding the art of a Professional School Counselor. He truly believes that *all* students should have every opportunity to succeed and reach their maximum potential.

Dr. Byrd previously served for the last ten years as the Department Chair for the Department of Secondary Education and School Leadership at Norfolk State University (NSU) where he oversaw graduate programs for students interested in pursuing their Master's Degree. He also served eight years as the NCATE/CAEP Coordinator for the School of Education. He is the Director of the Male Symposium that is held annually at Norfolk State University. He is also a member of the University Curriculum Committee and the co advisor of the under graduation chapter of Alpha Phi Alpha Fraternity at NSU. Dr. Byrd has authored and co-authored professional publications on the effects of African Americans in Higher Education, and academic advising styles preferred by African Americans; along with numerous professional presentations. In the community, he serves on several boards: Centura College Corporate Advisory Board, Blocker Norfolk YMCA Program Action Team Advisory Committee, and Board member for the Hampton Roads School Counselor Leadership Team. Dr. Byrd earned his Ph.D. in Counselor Education from his alma mater; Virginia Tech and is the recipient of the Distinguished Faculty Award for Teaching at NSU in 2016.

Dr. Melendez O. Byrd's premise for his teaching philosophy in counselor education is relatively simple. It requires practical learning experiences to prepare future counselors for the rigorous demands, as well as the rewards of being a professional school counselor. While constantly being submerged within the educational arena, Dr. Byrd truly feels that he has the potential to influence hundreds of educators and future school counselors who will in turn influence hundreds of thousands of young minds. It is the thought of all those minds being cultivated and nurtured that drives him to want to have a notable impact on students; while developing their competencies and skills essential to becoming professional school counselors, advocates, and leaders in the 21st century. It is our responsibility and goal to prepare highly competent, compassionate, collaborative and committed leaders.

Keesha M. Kerns, Ph.D., LPC, NCC, ACS

Dr. Kerns, an Assistant Professor at Norfolk State University since 2016, has spent the majority of her career divided between working in the clinical arena, focusing on substance abuse, researching suicidality, and supporting counselor educators. She is committed to teaching, clinical counseling, school counseling and special education, community service, scholarship, and research.

Dr. Kerns believes that it is imperative that counselor educators foster students' critical, conceptual, and ethical thinking skills and nurture their development into solid and competent Professional Counselors. Her professional and personal ambitions are twofold in design, meaning while she strives to utilize her experiences, expertise and training to make a lasting and prolific impression on the educational experience of students, she also supports the professional growth of *all* graduate students who chose helping professions. She truly aspires to the belief that every student should have opportunities to maximize potential to achieve success in their chosen endeavors. She is an advocate for students entering the counseling field and a support for clinicians in the schools and community.

Dr. Kerns has served for the last twenty years as a board member for Freelance Outreach, a non-profit organization dedicated to assisting homeless veterans, sponsoring individuals in substance abuse recovery and rehabilitation, and developing workforce programs targeting low income and at-risk populations. In addition to her board duties, she oversees the development of educational programs for the organization. Dr. Kerns is also a founding board member of The New Me Inc., a non-profit organization dedicated youth projects in Charlotte, North Carolina and a board member of the Florida based Youth Against Substance Abuse. Recently, she decided to start her own non-profit organization, The Project Connection Foundation, which works to support the homeless in Hampton Roads through varies projects ranging from food and coat drives to collecting back to school supplies and Toys for Tots for families in need. She is a twenty year member of The Order of Eastern Star, an organization that provides scholarship and a myriad of community services.

Dr. Keesha M. Kerns is a Licensed Professional Counselor in the states of North Carolina and Virginia. She holds a Virginia Pupil Personnel license as a Professional School Counselor and a School Counseling license in North Carolina. She has been a National Certified Counselor for more than seventeen years and is a National Approved Clinical Supervisor. She earned her doctoral degree in Counseling and Supervision from Old Dominion University and both her Masters of Arts in Counseling and Adult Education and Bachelors of Arts in Psychology from East Carolina University. Her career includes experience in community mental health counseling, over ten years in school counseling in two states, and almost twenty years in nonprofit services with the substance abuse population. Dr. Kerns research interest include counseling ethics, perception of pain in relation to treatment bias, substance abuse recovery, narrative therapy and therapeutic testimonials, the effectiveness of therapeutic day treatment in public education, and suicidality in the military. She has been involved in research with the Military Research Suicide Consortium and plans to expand her research in substance abuse and ethical counseling practices.

PURPOSE

Exploring the New Role of the Clinical Mental Health Counselor: Vignettes for Best Practices in the Community is intended to extend the ability to analyze matters related to clients and facilitate the development of ethical analytical skills. Within this workbook case scenarios can be found that are designed to heighten awareness of realistic and hypothetical issues and the ethical challenges presented therein. Additionally, this workbook will enhance resolution strategies to ultimately help create a successful learning system that will involve collaborative efforts among all parties to benefit professional growth, current clients and any future clients, and personal growth as well. As a clinical mental health counselor, this workbook will help maximize valuable service to clients by:

- Using this book to assist with the daily role as a clinical mental health counselor.

- Opening the mind of a counselor to change, but holding on to their values.

- Digging deep into the vignettes to help counselors consider all avenues while consulting with colleagues.

- Researching and applying the ACA Code of Ethics.

- Pausing frequently to be challenge to think outside the box.

- Keeping notes as a counselor explores each scenario to seek clarity and understanding.

The vignettes are meant to challenge counselors, as well as to prepare them for real life situations. It is important to utilize this workbook for professional development opportunities to collaborate with colleagues or students to establish best practices polices for all.

KEY TERMS

Advocacy: Counselors act *with* and on *behalf of* their clients and others in their clients' environments.

Aspirational Ethics: Refer to the highest professional standards of conduct to which counselors can aspire.

Confidentiality: A professional's promise or contract to respect clients' privacy by not disclosing anything revealed during counseling, except under agreed upon conditions.

Community Standards (or *Mores*): Define what is considered reasonable behavior when a case involving malpractice is litigated. They vary on interdisciplinary, theoretical, and geographical basis.

Ethics: Beliefs held about what constitutes right conduct. Ethics are moral principles adopted by an individual or group to provide rules for right conduct.

Mandatory Ethics: Level of ethical functioning wherein counselors comply with minimal standards, acknowledging the basic "musts" and "must nots".

Morality: Internal perspective of right and proper conduct and involves an evaluation of actions on the basis of some broader cultural context or religious standard.

Principle Ethics: Focuses on moral issues with the goal of solving a particular dilemma and establishing a framework to guide future ethical thinking and behavior while asking "Is this situation unethical"?

Professionalism: Has some relationship to ethical behavior, yet it is possible to act unprofessionally and still not act unethically.

Reasonableness: The care that is ordinarily exercised by others practicing within that specialty in the professional community.

Values: Beliefs and attitudes that provide direction to everyday living.

Virtue Ethics: Focuses on character traits of the counselor and non-obligatory ideals that asks "Am I doing what is best for my client?"

INTRODUCTION

Exploring the new role of the Clinical Mental Health Counselor will be a true experience and will provide the perfect opportunity for to absorb, collaborate and cultivate with others when discussing and learning the best practices. As a clinical counselor there are tough ethical and legal scenarios that will be faced on a daily basis. The ultimate goal when working with a client is to make a significant impact on someone's future; but more importantly making a positive change in their life. These real-life, relatable vignettes within this workbook are intriguing and will prompt deeper thinking about utilizing best policy and researching the proper ethical codes and standards.

While our country and all cultures face a myriad of problems that are perplexing; our clinical counselors are faced with a multitude of ethical issues that did not exist a few years ago. Awareness and adherence to American Counseling Association (ACA) ethical codes is critical for mental health counselors to assist in appropriate ethical decision making. This workbook is designed to help graduate students in training, practicing clinicians and counselors as they learn to embrace ethical conflicts for clarity and understanding. Do not be afraid to be honest with colleagues and supervisors through open discussion the material in this book promotes. Discussions will foster a comprehensive coverage of ethical decision making.

The Role of the Clinician in the Community

The role of the clinician in the community is ever changing. As advocator, educator, and professional counselor, the role of a mental health clinician has changed significantly over the years and has developed into a unique and pivotal component in today's complex community mental health system. Every year, budget cuts and underfunding for community mental health programs requires community workers providing services to extend the limits of their training and experience to accommodate the needs of the growing mental health population in the community. Not too long ago the mental health worker was just a case manager that connected clients with resources in the community, which included inpatient, outpatient or residential. Case managers would talk with clients about their difficulties, but not officially provide therapeutic services. Previously, that was the job of the psychologist, psychiatrist or whatever resource the client was connected to explore their emotional underpinnings.

However, in the ever changing times, counseling is no longer limited to the scope of serving clients in inpatient, outpatient and residential settings. The evolution of the counseling profession has opened up multiple avenues in the community for direct client services. The needs of mental health in the community demand that clinicians no longer sit in an office providing community resources and referrals. Now the needs of clients must be met at ground zero, in the client's environment. To meet those needs, every one providing a service must be trained in clinical services. This training includes the eight core areas of curriculum as outlined by the Council for Accredited Counseling and Related Educational Programs (CACREP) which includes professional counseling orientation and ethical practice, social and cultural diversity, human growth and development, career development, counseling and helping relationships, group counseling and group work, assessment and testing, and research and program evaluation (cacrep.org/glossary/common-core-areas). The common core CACREP areas represent fundamental knowledge areas that are the pillars of clinical education in the counseling profession. With a clinical education augmented by experience, the community counselor has become an effective and much needed staple in delivering mental health services in the community.

As clinicians service the community, they inherit many roles: change agent, consultant, adviser, advocate, coordinator of community support systems, and sponsors of a system of services that promotes self-healing and wellness. Working with clients is multifaceted in that it involves the ability to support community needs, developing partnerships in creation and delivery of services, promoting outreach to community organization and increasing strategies to empower clients within the community. Community clinicians must keep in mind the client's rights and the key components of being ethical with a population that is often misunderstood, mistreated and underserved. The potential risks the next generation of clinicians face is how to address circumstances that challenge their education and experiences while remaining the utmost professional counselor.

It is important to address these challenges, while clinicians sharpen their ethical decision making skills to avoid consequences that may lead to malpractice or worse, death. Refining ethical decision making skills comes through continued training, consultation with colleagues, and supervision. But the most effective teacher is the training which comes through life experiences. The combination of experience and training helps foster clinician counselors to be most effective in the community. The purpose of this workbook is to heighten awareness of ethical challenges through use of hypothetical topics within the community that will extend the ability to analyze matters related to clients while facilitating the development of ethical decision making skills. When reviewing the vignettes it is highly suggested to use the ***Practitioner's Guide to Ethical Decision Making*** by H. Forster-Miller and T. Davis (2016 & 1996). The dilemmas counselors face often are complex, but by utilizing this seven-step ethical decision making model, many resources will be hands-on and consequential. The seven steps are

1. Identify the problem.
2. Apply the ACA Code of Ethics.
3. Determine nature and dimensions of dilemma.
4. Generate potential courses of action.
5. Consider potential consequences of each course of action for all parties involved.
6. Evaluate the selected course of action.
7. Implement you course of action.

BASIC MORAL PRINCIPLES

While working in counseling, there are basic principles that guide decision making in dealing with and for clients. In needing services, clients still must be respected as individuals who have the right to be involved in the decisions pertaining to their life. As counselors, it is understood the importance of facilitating information to help create a change for clients. The best interest of the client is always a main priority, no matter the counselor or the situation.

Autonomy

The basic meaning is the right to self-govern, independence, or the right to be free from control or influence. For a counselor it means to promote self-determination with clients. Clients have the right to be independent and make informed, un-coerced decisions in their own lives.

Beneficence

In general, the meaning is to do good for others. It has also been characterized as the duty to do and to maximize good. For a counselor, it is the duty to promote the well-being of clients

Non-maleficence

Based on research this term refers to non-harming action that inflict the least amount of harm for the most beneficial result. For counselors it is defined as promising to avoid doing harm to clients.

Justice

The common definition of justice is fairness in the way people are treated. In the counseling profession it means to be fair by giving equally to others and to treat others justly.

Fidelity

The legal description of the term is faithfulness to a cause, belief or individual as demonstrated by an unwavering and continued loyalty and support. For counselors it is the ability to keep these professional promises and to make realistic commitments to clients

Veracity

The layman's meaning is habitual truthfulness and accuracy. In the counseling profession it is best described as being truthful and deal honestly with clients

In the words of Haim Ginnott (1977):

"I have come to the frightening conclusion that I am the decisive element in the lives of my clients. It is my personal approach that creates the climate. It is my daily mood that makes the weather. As a Clinical Mental Health Counselor, I possess a tremendous power to make a person's life miserable or joyous. I can be a tool of torture or an instrument of inspiration. I possess tremendous power to make a client's life miserable or joyous. I can humiliate or humor, hurt or heal. In all situations, it is my response that decides whether a crisis will be escalated or de-escalated and a person feels humanized or de-humanized."

SECTION 2

VIGNETTES

"We have this hope as an anchor for the soul, firm and secure. It enters the inner sanctuary behind the curtain."

(Heb 6:19)

The Surgery: Exploratory Vignette #1

Your new client, Zoe, who started three sessions ago, has been diagnosed with Major Depressive Disorder (MDD), adult Attention Deficit and Hyperactivity Disorder (ADHD) and dyslexia. Her major complaints focus on parenting issues and marital discord with her frequently absent husband. She comes into the session anxious about her child's upcoming eye surgery. Half way into the session Zoe talks about how she is the cause of her child needing the surgery. She confesses she threw a fork at the child in anger four years ago and hit him in the eye. Now she is overwhelmed with guilt and depression over the consequence of her actions (medical bills, child struggling at school, permanently scarring her child, keeping secrets from husband).

Step 1: Identify the ethical dilemma(s).

Step 2: Choose the Counseling Moral principle that address(es) this situation.

Step 3: What courses of action need to be taken to in this scenario?

Bonus: Which ACA ethical code(s) could be used to address this predicament?

MENTAL HEALTH COUNSELOR VIGNETTES

Group Membership: Exploratory Vignette #2

A coworker asks you to come to her group not only to co-facilitate but also to help with a difficult member. During your first time attending the group you notice that one of her members is very vocal and spirited in his group participation. Your coworker is very short with him and devalues his input, almost condescending. You notice her whole body language changes when he speaks. After group you inquire about him and get the response that he is aggressive like most of them leaving you to wonder what is meant by "most of them".

The next group meeting you observe this same behavior and notice the quote-unquote difficult member displaying signs of frustration. You notice that some group members are treated differently than others meaning some are indulged when others are mistreated. After group you ask your coworker about the group behaviors, only to hear her make excuses for the behaviors of some and justify treatment of others. When you ask about the difficult group member the response you get is "All of them are aggressive. It's just in their nature". She goes on to explain how she does not want the participation of an angry African American male to ruin her group or hinder the progress of other members in the group. As a matter of fact, she is considering having him transferred to another group for the good of everyone.

Step 1: Identify the ethical dilemma(s).

Step 2: Choose the Counseling Moral principle that address(es) this situation.

Step 3: What courses of action need to be taken to in this scenario?

Bonus: Which ACA ethical code(s) could be used to address this predicament?

Age Appropriate: Exploratory Vignette #3

A single mother calls your agency to refer her son, Michael, for counseling. She is looking for a counselor that deals with clients with peculiar behaviors. She feels that her son at the age of 22, has strange behaviors around the house, most of which are sexually based. He is constantly engaging in self-pleasuring activities openly inside the home. The mother explains to you that he has no friends and finds it difficult to relate to people. Her son works as a part-time custodian at a middle school. You decide to take Michael on as a client. In your fourth session he shares with you that he is more attractive to young people in the 15-16 age range. He quickly adds that he is attractive to someone who is 19 years old but has the body of a 15-16 year old.

Step 1: Identify the ethical dilemma(s).

Step 2: Choose the Counseling Moral principle that address(es) this situation.

Step 3: What courses of action need to be taken to in this scenario?

Bonus: Which ACA ethical code(s) could be used to address this predicament?

After Hours: Exploratory Vignette #4

You have been working with the case managers at a local community service board for over a year. A few of the case managers are old college friends and neighborhood acquaintances. One of them invites you to an after-hours events with a large group of employees from the community service board. You forge strong professional bonds with quite a few of the people at the community service board after that event. The case managers even make referrals to your company because of knowing you and trust your company based on your professional behavior.

One day during group supervision you share with the group during check-in that the case managers treated you out for your birthday. You think nothing about the incident because it was just a group of friends hanging out doing self-care. Sometime later, you hear off handed comments around the office about how beneficial and profitable your friendships are. Before the end of the week your supervisor calls you in to talk about professional boundaries at which you rebuff as no issues were raised when referrals were being made and the company received clients, increasing the company's revenue.

Step 1: Identify the ethical dilemma(s).

Step 2: Choose the Counseling Moral principle that address(es) this situation.

Step 3: What courses of action need to be taken to in this scenario?

Bonus: Which ACA ethical code(s) could be used to address this predicament?

Debatable Future: Exploratory Vignette #5

As a doctoral student, you have to supervise counseling students in the master's level program. A student in your master's level supervision group is struggling. Her recordings are bland and her transcriptions are inaccurate. During group she does not understand some basic counseling concepts and the other students in the group note that fact in complaints during individual sessions with you. During one of her recordings, it is evident she gives clients advice and easily strays off topic during the session. As the semester progresses, her development is inconsistent even after a few one on one sessions with another doctoral student advisor. In one of her final recordings, she discloses to the client personal information that is explicit in nature and unacceptable. Being concerned, you check her grades and discuss her situation with your fellow colleagues in a meeting. You get mixed results from colleagues and faculty during the meeting about her skills and academic achievement. Professionally, you question her future as a counselor and wonder if further considerations are warranted.

Step 1: Identify the ethical dilemma(s).

Step 2: Choose the Counseling Moral principle that address(es) this situation.

Step 3: What courses of action need to be taken to in this scenario?

Bonus: Which ACA ethical code(s) could be used to address this predicament?

MENTAL HEALTH COUNSELOR VIGNETTES

Generational Curse: Exploratory Vignette #6

Your new client Nobe is a 13-year-old boy in the sixth grade. He has major anger issues. He is constantly acting up in school, he cusses out his classmates and teachers, and is constantly trying to pick fights with anyone. Nobe has punched a special education kid in the back of the head for accidently sneezing on him. His father is a Sergeant in the U.S. Marines and divorced his mom two years ago. The mother has full custody. Both parents meet with the principal and school counselor because administration is considering kicking him out of school. Sergeant Evans desperately brings Nobe to your private practice for help, without the mother's permission. The father admits to you that his son has the same anger issues that he has and he feels that this is a generational curse in his family, because his father was abusive as well.

Step 1: Identify the ethical dilemma(s).

Step 2: Choose the Counseling Moral principle that address(es) this situation.

Step 3: What courses of action need to be taken to in this scenario?

Bonus: Which ACA ethical code(s) could be used to address this predicament?

MENTAL HEALTH COUNSELOR VIGNETTES

Secret Crush: Exploratory Vignette #7

You and a fellow co-worker have two clients in the same house in an alternative relationship. Your client has been diagnosed as Schizoaffective and her girlfriend as Intermittent Explosive Anger Disorder, PTSD and Histrionic Personality Disorder. Your co-worker's client reports there is a problem in the household because your client told her girlfriend she has a crush on you. Now your co-worker's client is interrupting your sessions and is requesting to go on community outings with you and your client; not her own worker. Your client's girlfriend vindictively called your supervisor to complain in an attempt to get her girlfriend a new worker. You have made it perfectly clear to your supervisor, the client's girlfriend and her worker that all you have is a professional relationship and are dedicated to working on your client's therapeutic needs. Now the girlfriend is threatening to call Medicaid and report that you "mistreated" her girlfriend by taking advantage of a person with a mental illness.

Step 1: Identify the ethical dilemma(s).

Step 2: Choose the Counseling Moral principle that address(es) this situation.

Step 3: What courses of action need to be taken to in this scenario?

Bonus: Which ACA ethical code(s) could be used to address this predicament?

MENTAL HEALTH COUNSELOR VIGNETTES

Other Worker: Exploratory Vignette #8

Nichel is a transfer client from another agency. Her diagnosis is Schizophrenia Undifferentiated type. The client reports she left her last agency because she could not trust her worker. Within the first week, Nichel has pushed the boundaries of the client/worker relationship by requesting you do all kinds of things from loaning her money to taking her to see her husband in jail. When you refused, she became distant and standoffish. She refused to keep her appointments for the rest of the week. A week later she offered to sell you her TV for money but would not tell you why she needed the money. The first of the month came and she needed to get to the drugstore for medication refills. The next day Nichel asks, did you want half of her prescription to sell like her other worker. She says her other worker would sell her medication and give her half of the money. Flabbergasted you refuse and emphasize the purpose of your sessions are to help with more than her finances. Nichel complains you are not addressing her needs and shuts down. At the end of the month she threatens to call your supervisor because the services are not working for her. She claims you are not her "type" of worker and wants a worker who understands her needs.

Step 1: Identify the ethical dilemma(s).

Step 2: Choose the Counseling Moral principle that address(es) this situation.

Step 3: What courses of action need to be taken to in this scenario?

Bonus: Which ACA ethical code(s) could be used to address this predicament?

MENTAL HEALTH COUNSELOR VIGNETTES

Social Suicide: Exploratory Vignette #9

For the last four years, you have been a specialist in suicide counseling. You are highly involved in the community and are often receiving counseling referrals for depression and suicide. While walking in the local mall, you see one of your previous clients Larry from three years ago who was vastly contemplating suicide. He is so excited to see you, he picks you up and gives you a hug and a big kiss on the cheek to thank you for saving his life. Larry truly believes that God sent you to him, to save his life. He feels that God is the answer to everyone's prayer. You also remember Larry for being savvy in technology and very active in social media. He takes out his phone and invites you to follow him on WhatsApp, TikTok, Twitter and Facebook. Larry wants to help promote you and share the good news about your services. He also wants to know if you two, together, can start a support group for individuals recovering from suicide. While in the mall Larry wants to treat you to Starbucks.

Step 1: Identify the ethical dilemma(s).

Step 2: Choose the Counseling Moral principle that address(es) this situation.

Step 3: What courses of action need to be taken to in this scenario?

Bonus: Which ACA ethical code(s) could be used to address this predicament?

The Election: Exploratory Vignette #10

Your new client, Vicky, was assigned to you after her mental health skill building (MHSB) worker went out sick unexpectedly. You will be working with this client for the next month. After a week she feels more comfortable and begins talking about the upcoming May election. You try not to discuss politics or candidates because it may influence the client's decision. When Vicky brings up the subject again, this time she wants to make sure you will take her to the polls because her other worker did not want to take her to vote in the last election as she was voting for the democratic ticket. After a heated discussion, the other worker finally did take her but wanted to go in the booth to make sure she voted for the republican. The poll worker did not let that happen. Shortly after they left the polls the other worker quizzed Vicky about who she voted for and reminded the client that if she did not vote "the right way" her services might be affected. As the client spoke, you noticed her body language changed just remembering the situation. You assure Vicky that will not happen and address the emotions you see the client experiencing. The client engages with you more after the election discussion and after the election itself expresses that she wants to stay on as one of your clients.

Step 1: Identify the ethical dilemma(s).

Step 2: Choose the Counseling Moral principle that address(es) this situation.

Step 3: What courses of action need to be taken to in this scenario?

Bonus: Which ACA ethical code(s) could be used to address this predicament?

New Agency: Exploratory Vignette #11

After years of working with a company, you transfer to another agency to work. Your clients want to go with you of their own free will; which is understandable, as you have worked with them for years. You know each client's diagnosis that will qualify them for services, no matter the agency. At the new agency the supervisor submitted the service authorization without all of the clients' diagnoses. The client got approved but you cannot write the individual service plan to appropriately address the client's need because some of the goals to deal with the client's diagnoses and symptoms were omitted. You were not allowed to see the new authorization before it was submitted. You want an explanation on what happened or why the authorization was submitted to create such a limited service plan. You think something questionable was done but your supervisor assures you the process was done correctly. She emphasizes that the agency always does what is best for the client.

Step 1: Identify the ethical dilemma(s).

Step 2: Choose the Counseling Moral principle that address(es) this situation.

Step 3: What courses of action need to be taken to in this scenario?

Bonus: Which ACA ethical code(s) could be used to address this predicament?

MENTAL HEALTH COUNSELOR VIGNETTES

Craving: Exploratory Vignette #12

For two months you have been counseling someone that feels highly confused, embarrassed and stressed with their constant need to engage in online dating. Your client is very attractive, and you enjoy how they smell every time they walk by you. Currently they are on ten different dating sites, Zoosk, Match, OurTime, Elite Single, Eharmony, BeNaughty, QuickFlirt, LoveBeginSat, Naughtydate, and Flirt. Your client has been extremely open with you while informing you on everything that happens every week. They even lightheartedly shared with you that they had a dream about you, but did not go into detail. Your client's conscience is heavy because they have shared with you that they have even slept with a married pastor of a church. You client admits that they have abnormally excessive and uncontrollable sexual desires. You have noticed within the last month that you look forward to hearing their either romantic or exotic scenarios that happens every weekend.

Step 1: Identify the ethical dilemma(s).

Step 2: Choose the Counseling Moral principle that address(es) this situation.

Step 3: What courses of action need to be taken to in this scenario?

Bonus: Which ACA ethical code(s) could be used to address this predicament?

The Stalker: Exploratory Vignette #13

As an instructor you design your counseling classes as a platform to model self-disclosure, as self-disclosure is a skill taught in the counseling profession. You have always promoted your classes as a safe place to share ideas, problems, and situations for feedback from faculty and peers. During the semester when others are self-disclosing, one particular student is super reserved and talks more about the job and clients rather than her professional growth. During one class she shares that she is a victim of stalking. At the end of the semester she request a meeting with you. In the meeting she explains the situation that she is being stalked and has been for eight months. The student goes on to tell you that to protect herself she has obtained a concealed weapons permit. You questioned her about carrying the weapon with her and if she has it on her now during the meeting. She replies that the university is an open area and she constantly receives message about crimes committed near or on the campus. She emphasizes that she feels the need to constantly protect herself as the local authorities are limited in what they can do to help her.

Step 1: Identify the ethical dilemma(s).

Step 2: Choose the Counseling Moral principle that address(es) this situation.

Step 3: What courses of action need to be taken to in this scenario?

Bonus: Which ACA ethical code(s) could be used to address this predicament?

The Neighbor: Exploratory Vignette #14

One dark and stormy night, there is a knock at your door. Your neighbor and child's teammate, Myles, is standing outside crying. He says his father punched him and he just had to leave the house. Your son's friend knows that you are a counselor and asks can he stay until the troubles at his house blow over. Knowing the laws and not wanting to harbor a runaway, you agree for the moment. You also are worried about the child because he has some behavioral issues. Later that evening you watch to see if the police arrive at Myles' house or if his parents are looking for him. By one in the morning nothing has happened. The next morning you call the school and speak to the junior class counselor. She tells you that Myles' parents have not contacted the school to report him missing and he is present in school today. Your call was the first time she heard anything was wrong and now must consult with school administration. His school counselor is concerned and ask how are you going to handle this matter.

Step 1: Identify the ethical dilemma(s).

Step 2: Choose the Counseling Moral principle that address(es) this situation.

Step 3: What courses of action need to be taken to in this scenario?

Bonus: Which ACA ethical code(s) could be used to address this predicament?

MENTAL HEALTH COUNSELOR VIGNETTES

#helpme: Exploratory Vignette #15

Arthur and Keke have been in a relationship for over three years now and are attending couples counseling, since they moved in together eight months ago. In the second session you ask for more information about the type of fights that they are having. Keke shares with you that Arthur has smacked her into the door, but he claims that he only pushed her head and shoulder into the door. Arthurs reports that he was in self-defense because Keke was hitting him with a broom first. Arthur states that Keke is extremely jealous and is always checking his phone because she believes he is cheating on her. Keke also reports that Arthur forced her to have sex while she was on her period. He admits that both were drunk that night and he does not remember. Arthur has even tried to leave Keke but she did not want him to leave. Arthur even admits that one night they both got so mad with each other that he pulled a gun out and threatened to kill himself, just so she would stop nagging him.

Step 1: Identify the ethical dilemma(s).

Step 2: Choose the Counseling Moral principle that address(es) this situation.

Step 3: What courses of action need to be taken to in this scenario?

Bonus: Which ACA ethical code(s) could be used to address this predicament?

The Company: Exploratory Vignette #16

Your old coworker has opened his own agency. You are happy for him and flattered he asked you to work with him doing community mental health assessments. During training you observe one skill building assessment and when the housing section of the assessment comes up the assessor says the client will live in one of the houses owned by your friend's partner company. You inquire about that situation later and the assessor's response is that people in certain halfway houses must utilize the agency's services. You refute that by reminding the assessors that clients' have a choice in everything, including the service provider. He responds by asking if you want to keep your job working at the agency or not because he is close friends with the owner and will report your questioning behavior.

Step 1: Identify the ethical dilemma(s).

Step 2: Choose the Counseling Moral principle that address(es) this situation.

Step 3: What courses of action need to be taken to in this scenario?

Bonus: Which ACA ethical code(s) could be used to address this predicament?

MENTAL HEALTH COUNSELOR VIGNETTES

Oh Bedbugs: Exploratory Vignette #17

One of your regular clients, Nella, lives at an assisted living facility. One unassuming afternoon, you drop off Nella from a medication management appointment and the nursing assistant on staff tells you that you cannot go to her room because the facility has bedbugs. She suggest that you put your clothes in the dryer when you get home to make sure none were alive on your clothes. You immediately call your supervisor to report the information. She tells you to stop seeing the client until the facility is cleared. You contact the client's community service board case manager to let her know services will be suspended until the bedbug situation is cleared. The case manager contacts the client's day treatment and now the client cannot go to day treatment due to the possibility of spreading bedbugs. The facility manager calls you when the client has a psychotic behavior episode because her schedule was interrupted. You explain the supervisor's directive and tell them to notify the company when the bedbugs are gone. The facility manager tells you that she is going to contact the site director because you are unprofessional and broke a client's confidentiality.

Step 1: Identify the ethical dilemma(s).

Step 2: Choose the Counseling Moral principle that address(es) this situation.

Step 3: What courses of action need to be taken to in this scenario?

Bonus: Which ACA ethical code(s) could be used to address this predicament?

MENTAL HEALTH COUNSELOR VIGNETTES

Mister Fixit: Exploratory Vignette #18

Two days ago, you dropped your car off at Joshua's Honest Auto to get repaired. Your new client Joshua the owner and local mechanic comes to your office extremely depressed that his daughter is contemplating suicide. Joshua automatically remembers you from two days ago, because he is still working on your car. He informs you that he walked in on his 18-year-old daughter while having sex with a black man. He admits to you that he is prejudice, belongs to a hate group and would like for you to counsel his daughter. Joshua also confesses that he is unable to pay for the counseling sessions that you recommended because his money is currently caught up with the IRS and he acknowledges that he has a gambling problem. He desperately rambles off that he will paint, change the oil, fix your car or give you new tires; whatever you need. Joshua is desperate and pleads that he just wants you to help his daughter. He said if his daughter killed herself, he would go crazy and kill that black man, as well as himself. Joshua cries out for your help.

Step 1: Identify the ethical dilemma(s).

Step 2: Choose the Counseling Moral principle that address(es) this situation.

Step 3: What courses of action need to be taken to in this scenario?

Bonus: Which ACA ethical code(s) could be used to address this predicament?

Personal Planner: Exploratory Vignette #19

You have been working in community services with clients with axis I & II diagnosis for almost ten years. Last year you were assigned a client with severe auditory and visual hallucinations. He talked about them daily and one of the goals on his individual service plan (ISP) was to help him develop coping skills to deal with his hallucinations. He has dealt with them with using journaling and adult coloring books with some success. For the most part, he is making progress on all his goals.

Three weeks ago, he was arrested and charged with murder. Because he has a mental illness and a community counselor, the detectives call you in for questioning concerning his whereabouts at the time of the murders and mental state. With legal assistance from your supervisor, you answer all questions until they ask about any notes from your sessions with the client.

You are hesitant because there are two sets of notes, ones for his file and your personal planner which has other clients' information as well as your personal appointments. You turn to your supervisor who says that legally you have to give them up because the client is a danger to himself and/or others.

Step 1: Identify the ethical dilemma(s).

Step 2: Choose the Counseling Moral principle that address(es) this situation.

Step 3: What courses of action need to be taken to in this scenario?

Bonus: Which ACA ethical code(s) could be used to address this predicament?

MENTAL HEALTH COUNSELOR VIGNETTES

Petty Repercussions: Exploratory Vignette #20

Previously your company dealt with clients from a local assisted living facility having bedbugs. The facility management was unhappy feeling like the situation was mishandled and has been banned anyone from your company from seeing clients. Clients are not showing up for medical, medication management or therapy appointments. The company has received multiple complaints from clients, case managers and providers because clients are not receiving services. During this time a client served by your company missed a medical appointment and did not get a refill on her hypertension medication. Later that week the client suffered a stroke and had to be moved into a rehabilitation facility. She is now permanently partial paralyzed and after rehabilitation will be sent back to the same assisted living facility. The client is requesting her rights to see her worker from the company even in rehab facility Upon the client's request, the nurses call the company to ask the worker to continue services in rehab.

Step 1: Identify the ethical dilemma(s).

Step 2: Choose the Counseling Moral principle that address(es) this situation.

Step 3: What courses of action need to be taken to in this scenario?

Bonus: Which ACA ethical code(s) could be used to address this predicament?

Running Confessions: Exploratory Vignette #21

This is your second session with the Catholic preacher. You feel a little uncomfortable because the first session seemed odd and you felt that he was not being honest with you. You even consulted with a colleague on how you felt in the first session with the preacher because you wanted to seek personal and professional advice. When he sits in your office for his second session you noticed that his face is flushed with a slight perspiration. From your observation he seems perplexed and extremely nervous. The Catholic preacher opens up to you about confidentiality and how he understands it works within the confines of his church. He wants to talk to you about what he has witnessed within the church, as well as participated in, but wants to know if you will notify the police. After asking the question, he observes your non-verbals and runs out the office.

Step 1: Identify the ethical dilemma(s).

Step 2: Choose the Counseling Moral principle that address(es) this situation.

Step 3: What courses of action need to be taken to in this scenario?

Bonus: Which ACA ethical code(s) could be used to address this predicament?

New Girlfriend: Exploratory Vignette #22

Your client Keith that has been diagnosed with Dysthymia calls to ask you to pick him up from his new girlfriend's house. He talks about his new girlfriend for a week or more. He seems very happy and wants to really work on his goals to be a better person for this new girlfriend. Keith even hints they have become intimate recently. On the day you are introduced to the new girlfriend, the girlfriend recognizes your agency and says she has a worker there as well. She tells you the worker's name and you are puzzled because the agency does not allow female clients to have male workers. You see your co-worker at the next staff meeting and mention about encountering his female client. The co-worker reports that he does not have a female client, but a transitioning transgender client that is dating a new guy whom he has not disclosed his sexual orientation or situation.

Step 1: Identify the ethical dilemma(s).

Step 2: Choose the Counseling Moral principle that address(es) this situation.

Step 3: What courses of action need to be taken to in this scenario?

Bonus: Which ACA ethical code(s) could be used to address this predicament?

MENTAL HEALTH COUNSELOR VIGNETTES

Baby Drama: Exploratory Vignette #23

Your client, Norma, has been diagnosed with Bi Polar II, PTSD and Substance Use Disorder-Cocaine Use and HIV. She has been with you less than three months and her cooperation in sessions has been minimal. During that time she has barely managed her money and her abusive long distance boyfriend badgers her to take money out of the household to send to him. Norma is raising her five children and four dogs on a budget of less than $2000 a month. She will not take any medication because she does not trust her psychiatrist; or that is what she tells you. After weeks of inquiring about taking medication, she tells you she thinks she is pregnant. This will be her sixth child. Norma refuses to go to the doctor because she claims her pregnancies are hard to detect. After another week she tells you she does not know who the father is because she has slept with three or four different men including her neighbor. She discloses to you that she told the men she has the virus and they are "cool with it as long as the baby is theirs". Norma has now taken money from all three to help her household, but refuses to confirm her pregnancy.

Step 1: Identify the ethical dilemma(s).

Step 2: Choose the Counseling Moral principle that address(es) this situation.

Step 3: What courses of action need to be taken to in this scenario?

Bonus: Which ACA ethical code(s) could be used to address this predicament?

Misrepresenting Letters: Exploratory Vignette #24

You are at a conference where you see old classmates from your graduate program. One classmate, Rick, is presenting on an interesting subject, so you decide to support him by attending his presentation. His presentation is full of questionable facts and misrepresentations and you notice his credentials look a little strange. At lunch with other classmates you mention the presentation and the group responds with groans and eye rolling. Another classmate even comments on Rick being "the same liar in a different job". Puzzled you dig deeper into these present reactions as you remember the classmate in question being reserved but generally a good person. You find out that your former classmate, Rick, is misrepresenting his credentials on purpose as he graduated from an accredited program. He knows the regulations and how deceitful presentation of credentials is wrong. Other classmates in the lunch group that have worked with him in the past say he misrepresents himself for promotion purposes and that his reputation in the community is that he is fraudulent, lazy and unqualified.

Step 1: Identify the ethical dilemma(s).

Step 2: Choose the Counseling Moral principle that address(es) this situation.

Step 3: What courses of action need to be taken to in this scenario?

Bonus: Which ACA ethical code(s) could be used to address this predicament?

MENTAL HEALTH COUNSELOR VIGNETTES

Estranged Marriage: Exploratory Vignette #25

You are assigned to a preexisting in-home case with three other workers. Your 14 year old client was molested by the mother's husband who was recently released from prison for the conviction. Two weeks into working with the client you do a home session and a large man walks into the room. He does not speak but your client makes a noticeable body language change. Her body language becomes withdrawn and she shuts down. You suggest taking a walk outside and she eagerly agrees. Once outside she relaxes and talks about school and dealing with peers. At the end of the session you walk back in the home and the client wants to sit outside. You get this approved by the mother and document the interactions of the entire session.

During the next session you find out the large man was the person that molested your client. He has been court ordered not to be around the client, but the mother insist she is working on their estranged marriage. You are in session again when the man walks in acting strange. Before he has seemingly ignored you but today he approaches you. He looks at you but says nothing. He walks in the kitchen and says loudly "I don't like strangers in my business" before he slams the door.

Step 1: Identify the ethical dilemma(s).

Step 2: Choose the Counseling Moral principle that address(es) this situation.

Step 3: What courses of action need to be taken to in this scenario?

Bonus: Which ACA ethical code(s) could be used to address this predicament?

SECTION 3

CREATE YOUR OWN VIGNETTES

INSTRUCTIONS

1) CREATE YOUR OWN EXPLORATORY VIGNETTES
2) SHARE WITH THE GROUP

This assignment involves the development of your own ethical dilemmas that can be utilize in a community setting. Create a dilemma that challenges counseling professionals and fosters the application of critical thinking skills. How will this scenario reflect one of the ethical principles? What ACA codes will your scenario fall under? How will the scenario promote counselors to act in an ethical manner? How will this scenario foster professionalism? Feel free to be inventive, original, artistic, resourceful, visionary, and inspirational. Created dilemma should help the irrational, become rational, the unethical become ethical, the unprofessional become professional, and the incompetent become competent.

MENTAL HEALTH COUNSELOR VIGNETTES

Create Your Own Exploratory Vignette Title: _____

_____
_____
_____
_____
_____
_____
_____
_____

Step 1: Identify the ethical dilemma(s).

Step 2: Choose the Counseling Moral principle that address(es) this situation.

Step 3: What courses of action need to be taken to in this scenario?

Bonus: Which ACA ethical code(s) could be used to address this predicament?

Create Your Own Exploratory Vignette Title: _____

_____
_____
_____
_____
_____
_____
_____
_____

Step 1: Identify the ethical dilemma(s).

Step 2: Choose the Counseling Moral principle that address(es) this situation.

Step 3: What courses of action need to be taken to in this scenario?

Bonus: Which ACA ethical code(s) could be used to address this predicament?

Create Your Own Exploratory Vignette Title: _____

_____
_____
_____
_____
_____
_____
_____
_____

Step 1: Identify the ethical dilemma(s).

Step 2: Choose the Counseling Moral principle that address(es) this situation.

Step 3: What courses of action need to be taken to in this scenario?

Bonus: Which ACA ethical code(s) could be used to address this predicament?

Create Your Own Exploratory Vignette Title: _____

_____
_____
_____
_____
_____
_____
_____
_____

Step 1: Identify the ethical dilemma(s).

Step 2: Choose the Counseling Moral principle that address(es) this situation.

Step 3: What courses of action need to be taken to in this scenario?

Bonus: Which ACA ethical code(s) could be used to address this predicament?

MENTAL HEALTH COUNSELOR VIGNETTES

Create Your Own Exploratory Vignette Title: _____

_____
_____
_____
_____
_____
_____
_____
_____

Step 1: Identify the ethical dilemma(s).

Step 2: Choose the Counseling Moral principle that address(es) this situation.

Step 3: What courses of action need to be taken to in this scenario?

Bonus: Which ACA ethical code(s) could be used to address this predicament?

SECTION 4

APPENDIX

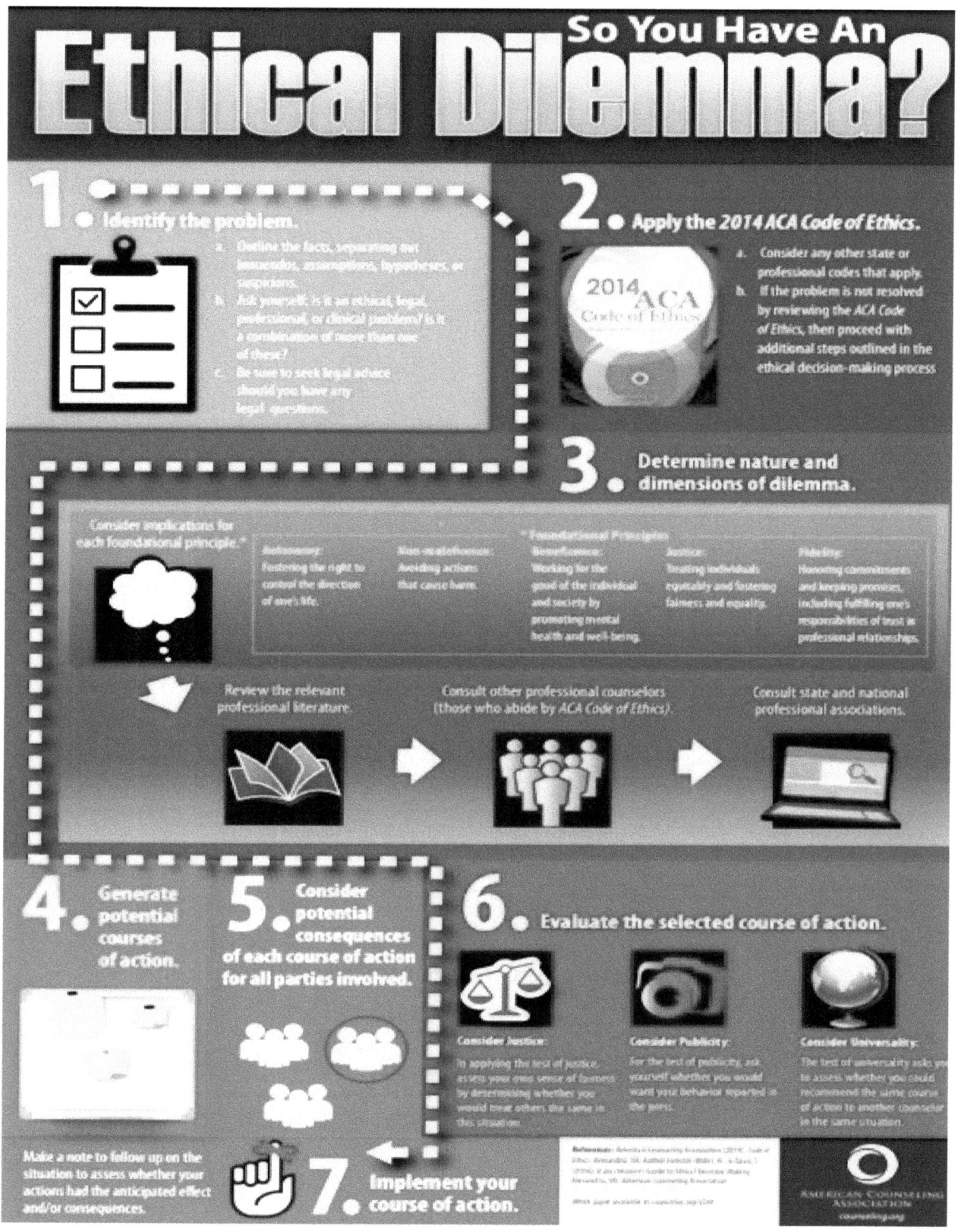

2014 ACA Code of Ethics

As approved by the ACA Governing Council

AMERICAN COUNSELING ASSOCIATION

counseling.org

Mission

The mission of the American Counseling Association is to enhance the quality of life in society by promoting the development of professional counselors, advancing the counseling profession, and using the profession and practice of counseling to promote respect for human dignity and diversity.

© 2014 by the American Counseling Association.

Contents

ACA Code of Ethics Preamble

ACA Code of Ethics Purpose

Section A

   The Counseling Relationship

Section B

   Confidentiality and Privacy

Section C

   Professional Responsibility

Section D

   Relationships With Other Professionals

Section E

   Evaluation, Assessment, and Interpretation

Section F

   Supervision, Training, and Teaching

Section G

   Research and Publication

Section H

   Distance Counseling, Technology, and Social Media

Section I

   Resolving Ethical Issues

   Glossary of Terms

   Index

ACA Code of Ethics Preamble

The American Counseling Association (ACA) is an educational, scientific, and professional organization whose members work in a variety of settings and serve in multiple capacities. Counseling is a professional relationship that empowers diverse individuals, families, and groups to accomplish mental health, wellness, education, and career goals.

Professional values are an important way of living out an ethical commitment. The following are core professional values of the counseling profession:

1. enhancing human development throughout the life span;
2. honoring diversity and embracing a multicultural approach in support of the worth, dignity, potential, and uniqueness of people within their social and cultural contexts;
3. promoting social justice;
4. safeguarding the integrity of the counselor–client relationship; and
5. practicing in a competent and ethical manner.

These professional values provide a conceptual basis for the ethical principles enumerated below. These principles are the foundation for ethical behavior and decision making. The fundamental principles of professional ethical behavior are

- *autonomy*, or fostering the right to control the direction of one's life;
- *nonmaleficence*, or avoiding actions that cause harm;
- *beneficence*, or working for the good of the individual and society by promoting mental health and well-being;
- *justice*, or treating individuals equitably and fostering fairness and equality;
- *fidelity*, or honoring commitments and keeping promises, including fulfilling one's responsibilities of trust in professional relationships; and
- *veracity*, or dealing truthfully with individuals with whom counselors come into professional contact.

ACA Code of Ethics Purpose

The *ACA Code of Ethics* serves six main purposes:

1. The *Code* sets forth the ethical obligations of ACA members and provides guidance intended to inform the ethical practice of professional counselors.
2. The *Code* identifies ethical considerations relevant to professional counselors and counselors-in-training.
3. The *Code* enables the association to clarify for current and prospective members, and for those served by members, the nature of the ethical responsibilities held in common by its members.
4. The *Code* serves as an ethical guide designed to assist members in constructing a course of action that best serves those utilizing counseling services and establishes expectations of conduct with a primary emphasis on the role of the professional counselor.
5. The *Code* helps to support the mission of ACA.
6. The standards contained in this *Code* serve as the basis for processing inquiries and ethics

complaints concerning ACA members.

The *ACA Code of Ethics* contains nine main sections that ad- dress the following areas:

Section A: The Counseling Relationship

Section B: Confidentiality and Privacy Section

C: Professional Responsibility

Section D: Relationships With Other Professionals

Section E: Evaluation, Assessment, and Interpretation

Section F: Supervision, Training, and Teaching

Section G: Research and Publication

Section H: Distance Counseling, Technology, and Social Media

Section I: Resolving Ethical Issues

Each section of the *ACA Code of Ethics* begins with an introduction. The introduction to each section describes the ethical behavior and responsibility to which counselors aspire. The introductions help set the tone for each particular section and provide a starting point that invites reflection on the ethical standards contained in each part of the *ACA Code of Ethics*. The standards outline professional responsibilities and provide direction for fulfilling those ethical responsibilities.

When counselors are faced with ethical dilemmas that are difficult to resolve, they are expected to engage in a care- fully considered ethical decision-making process, consulting available resources as needed. Counselors acknowledge that resolving ethical issues is a process; ethical reasoning includes consideration of professional values, professional ethical principles, and ethical standards.

Counselors' actions should be consistent with the spirit as well as the letter of these ethical standards. No specific ethical decision-making model is always most effective, so counselors are expected to use a credible model of decision making that can bear public scrutiny of its application. Through a chosen ethical decision-making process and evaluation of the context of the situation, counselors work collaboratively with clients to make decisions that promote clients' growth and development. A breach of the standards and principles provided herein does not necessarily constitute legal liability or violation of the law; such action is established in legal and judicial proceedings.

The glossary at the end of the *Code* provides a concise description of some of the terms used in the *ACA Code of Ethics*.

Section A

The Counseling Relationship

Introduction

Counselors facilitate client growth and development in ways that foster the interest and welfare of clients and promote formation of healthy relationships. Trust is the cornerstone of the counseling relationship, and counselors have the responsibility to respect and safeguard the client's right to privacy and confidentiality. Counselors actively attempt to understand the diverse cultural backgrounds of the clients they serve. Counselors also explore their own cultural identities and how these affect their values and beliefs about the counseling process. Additionally, counselors are encouraged to contribute to society by devoting a portion of their professional activities for little or no financial return (*pro bono publico*).

A.1. Client Welfare

A.1.a. Primary Responsibility

The primary responsibility of counselors is to respect the dignity and promote the welfare of clients.

A.1.b. Records and Documentation

Counselors create, safeguard, and maintain documentation necessary for rendering professional services. Regardless of the medium, counselors include sufficient and timely documentation to facilitate the delivery and continuity of services. Counselors take reasonable steps to ensure that documentation accurately reflect client progress and services provided. If amendments are made to records and documentation, counselors take steps to properly note the amendments according to agency or institutional policies.

A.1.c. Counseling Plans

Counselors and their clients work jointly in devising counseling plans that offer reasonable promise of success and are consistent with the abilities, temperament, developmental level, and circumstances of clients. Counselors and clients regularly review and revise counseling plans to assess their continued viability and effectiveness, respecting clients' freedom of choice.

A.1.d. Support Network Involvement

Counselors recognize that support networks hold various meanings in the lives of clients and consider enlisting the support, understanding, and involvement of others (e.g., religious/spiritual/community leaders, family members, friends) as positive resources, when appropriate, with client consent.

A.2. Informed Consent in the Counseling Relationship

A.2.a. Informed Consent

Clients have the freedom to choose whether to enter into or remain in a counseling relationship and need adequate information about the counseling process and the counselor. Counselors have an obligation to re- view in writing and verbally with clients the rights and responsibilities of both counselors and clients. Informed consent is an ongoing part of the counseling process, and counselors appropriately document discussions of informed consent throughout the counseling relationship.

A.2.b. Types of Information Needed

Counselors explicitly explain to clients the nature of all services provided. They inform clients about issues such as, but not limited to, the following: the purposes, goals, techniques, procedures, limitations, potential risks, and benefits of services; the counselor's qualifying credentials, relevant experience, and approach to counseling; continuation of services upon the incapacitation or death of the counselor; the role of technology; and other pertinent information. Counselors take steps to ensure that clients understand the implications of diagnosis and the intended use of tests and reports. Additionally, counselors inform clients about fees and billing arrangements, including procedures for nonpayment of fees. Clients have the right to confidentiality and to be provided with an explanation of its limits (including how supervisors and/or treatment or interdisciplinary team professionals are involved), to obtain clear information about their records, to participate in the ongoing counseling plans, and to refuse any services or modality changes and to be advised of the consequences of such refusal.

A.2.c. Developmental and Cultural Sensitivity

Counselors communicate information in ways that are both developmentally and culturally appropriate. Counselors use clear and understandable language when discussing issues related to informed consent. When clients have difficulty understanding the language that counselors use, counselors provide necessary services (e.g., arranging for a qualified interpreter or translator) to ensure comprehension by clients. In collaboration with clients, counselors consider cultural implications of informed consent procedures and, where possible, counselors adjust their practices accordingly.

A.2.d. Inability to Give Consent

When counseling minors, incapacitated adults, or other persons unable to give voluntary consent, counselors seek the assent of clients to services and include them in decision making as appropriate. Counselors recognize the need to balance the ethical rights of clients to make choices, their capacity to give consent or assent to receive services, and parental or familial legal rights and responsibilities to protect these clients and make decisions on their behalf.

A.2.e. Mandated Clients

Counselors discuss the required limitations to confidentiality when working with clients who have been mandated for counseling services. Counselors also explain what type of information and with whom that information is shared prior to the beginning of counseling. The client may choose to refuse services. In this case, counselors will, to the best of their ability, discuss with the client the potential consequences of refusing counseling services.

A.3. Clients Served by Others

When counselors learn that their clients are in a professional relationship with other mental health professionals, they request release from clients to inform the other professionals and strive to establish positive and collaborative professional relationships.

A.4. Avoiding Harm and Imposing Values

A.4.a. Avoiding Harm

Counselors act to avoid harming their clients, trainees, and research participants and to minimize or to remedy unavoidable or unanticipated harm.

A.4.b. Personal Values

Counselors are aware of—and avoid imposing—their own values, attitudes, beliefs, and behaviors. Counselors respect the diversity of clients, trainees, and research participants and seek training in areas in which they are at risk of imposing their values onto clients, especially when the counselor's values are inconsistent with the client's goals or are discriminatory in nature.

A.5. Prohibited Noncounseling Roles and Relationships

A.5.a. Sexual and/or Romantic Relationships Prohibited

Sexual and/or romantic counselor–client interactions or relationships with current clients, their romantic partners, or their family members are prohibited. This prohibition applies to both in-person and electronic interactions or relationships.

A.5.b. Previous Sexual and/or Romantic Relationships

Counselors are prohibited from engaging in counseling relationships with persons with whom they have had a previous sexual and/or romantic relationship.

A.5.c. Sexual and/or Romantic Relationships With Former Clients

Sexual and/or romantic counselor–client interactions or relationships with former clients, their romantic partners, or their family members are prohibited for a period of 5 years following the last professional contact. This prohibition applies to both in-person and electronic interactions or relationships. Counselors, before engaging in sexual and/or romantic interactions or relationships with former clients, their romantic partners, or their family members, demonstrate forethought and document (in written form) whether the interaction or relationship can be viewed as exploitive in any way and/or whether there is still potential to harm the former client; in cases of potential exploitation and/or harm, the counselor avoids entering into such an interaction or relationship.

A.5.d. Friends or Family Members

Counselors are prohibited from engaging in counseling relationships with friends or family members with whom they have an inability to remain objective.

A.5.e. Personal Virtual Relationships With Current Clients

Counselors are prohibited from engaging in a personal virtual relationship with individuals with whom they have a current counseling relationship (e.g., through social and other media).

A.6. Managing and Maintaining Boundaries and Professional Relationships

A.6.a. Previous Relationships

Counselors consider the risks and benefits of accepting as clients those with whom they have had a previous relationship. These potential clients may include individuals with whom the counselor has had a casual, distant, or past relationship. Examples include mutual or past membership in a professional association, organization, or community. When counselors accept these clients, they take appropriate professional precautions such as informed consent, consultation, supervision, and documentation to ensure that judgment is not impaired and no exploitation occurs.

A.6.b. Extending Counseling Boundaries

Counselors consider the risks and benefits of extending current counseling relationships beyond conventional parameters. Examples include attending a client's formal ceremony (e.g., a wedding/commitment ceremony or graduation), purchasing a service or product provided by a client (excepting unrestricted bartering), and visiting a client's ill family member in the hospital. In extending these boundaries, counselors take appropriate professional precautions such as informed consent, consultation, supervision, and documentation to ensure that judgment is not impaired and no harm occurs.

A.6.c. Documenting Boundary Extensions

If counselors extend boundaries as described in A.6.a. and A.6.b., they must officially document, prior to the interaction (when feasible), the rationale for such an interaction, the potential benefit, and anticipated consequences for the client or former client and other individuals significantly involved with the client or former client. When unintentional harm occurs to the client or former client, or to an individual significantly involved with the client or former client, the counselor must show evidence of an attempt to remedy such harm.

A.6.d. Role Changes in the Professional Relationship

When counselors change a role from the original or most recent contracted relationship, they obtain informed consent from the client and explain the client's right to refuse services related to the change. Examples of role changes include, but are not limited to

1. changing from individual to relationship or family counseling, or vice versa;
2. changing from an evaluative role to a therapeutic role, or vice versa; and
3. changing from a counselor to a mediator role, or vice versa.

Clients must be fully informed of any anticipated consequences (e.g., financial, legal, personal, therapeutic) of counselor role changes.

A.6.e. Nonprofessional Interactions or Relationships (Other Than Sexual or Romantic Interactions or Relationships)

Counselors avoid entering into non-professional relationships with former clients, their romantic partners, or their family members when the interaction is potentially harmful to the client. This applies to both in-person and electronic interactions or relationships.

A.7. Roles and Relationships at Individual, Group, Institutional, and Societal Levels

A.7.a. Advocacy

When appropriate, counselors advocate at individual, group, institutional, and societal levels to address potential barriers and obstacles that inhibit access and/or the growth and development of clients.

A.7.b. Confidentiality and Advocacy

Counselors obtain client consent prior to engaging in advocacy efforts on behalf of an identifiable client to improve the provision of services and to work toward removal of systemic barriers or obstacles that inhibit client access, growth, and development.

A.8. Multiple Clients

When a counselor agrees to provide counseling services to two or more persons who have a relationship, the counselor clarifies at the outset which person or persons are clients and the nature of the relationships the counselor will have with each involved person. If it becomes apparent that the counselor may be called upon to perform potentially conflicting roles, the counselor will clarify, adjust, or withdraw from roles appropriately.

A.9. Group Work

A.9.a. Screening

Counselors screen prospective group counseling/therapy participants. To the extent possible, counselors select members whose needs and goals are compatible with the goals of the group, who will not impede the group process, and whose well-being will not be jeopardized by the group experience.

A.9.b. Protecting Clients

In a group setting, counselors take reasonable precautions to protect clients from physical, emotional, or psychological trauma.

A.10. Fees and Business Practices

A.10.a. Self-Referral

Counselors working in an organization (e.g., school, agency, institution) that provides counseling services do not refer clients to their private practice unless the policies of a particular organization make explicit provisions for self-referrals. In such instances, the clients must be informed of other options open to them should they seek private counseling services.

A.10.b. Unacceptable Business Practices

Counselors do not participate in fee splitting, nor do they give or receive commissions, rebates, or any other form of remuneration when referring clients for professional services.

A.10.c. Establishing Fees

In establishing fees for professional counseling services, counselors consider the financial status of clients and locality. If a counselor's usual fees create undue hardship for the client, the counselor may adjust fees, when legally permissible, or assist the client in locating comparable, affordable services.

A.10.d. Nonpayment of Fees

If counselors intend to use collection agencies or take legal measures to collect fees from clients who do not pay for services as agreed upon, they include such information in their informed consent documents and also inform clients in a timely fashion of intended actions and offer clients the opportunity to make payment.

A.10.e. Bartering

Counselors may barter only if the bartering does not result in exploitation or harm, if the client requests it, and if such arrangements are an accepted practice among professionals in the community. Counselors consider the cultural implications of bartering and discuss relevant concerns with clients and document such agreements in a clear written contract.

A.10.f. Receiving Gifts

Counselors understand the challenges of accepting gifts from clients and recognize that in some cultures, small gifts are a token of respect and gratitude. When determining whether to accept a gift from clients, counselors take into account the therapeutic relationship, the monetary value of the gift, the client's motivation for giving the gift, and the counselor's motivation for wanting to accept or decline the gift.

A.11. Termination and Referral

A.11.a. Competence Within Termination and Referral

If counselors lack the competence to be of professional assistance to clients, they avoid entering or continuing counseling relationships. Counselors are knowledgeable about culturally and clinically appropriate referral resources and suggest these alternatives. If clients decline the suggested referrals, counselors discontinue the relationship.

A.11.b. Values Within Termination and Referral

Counselors refrain from referring prospective and current clients based solely on the counselor's personally held values, attitudes, beliefs, and behaviors. Counselors respect the diversity of clients and seek training in areas in which they are at risk of imposing their values onto clients, especially when the counselor's values are inconsistent with the client's goals or are discriminatory in nature.

A.11.c. Appropriate Termination

Counselors terminate a counseling relationship when it becomes reasonably apparent that the client no longer needs assistance, is not likely to benefit or is being harmed by continued counseling. Counselors may terminate counseling when in jeopardy of harm by the client or by another person with whom the client has a relationship, or when clients do not pay fees as agreed upon. Counselors provide pre-termination counseling and recommend other service providers when necessary.

A.11.d. Appropriate Transfer of Services

When counselors transfer or refer clients to other practitioners, they ensure that appropriate clinical and administrative processes are completed and open communication is maintained with both clients and practitioners.

A.12. Abandonment and Client Neglect

Counselors do not abandon or neglect clients in counseling. Counselors assist in making appropriate arrangements for the continuation of treatment, when necessary, during interruptions such as vacations, illness, and following termination.

Section B
Confidentiality and Privacy

Introduction

Counselors recognize that trust is a cornerstone of the counseling relationship. Counselors aspire to earn the trust of clients by creating an ongoing partnership, establishing and upholding appropriate boundaries, and maintaining confidentiality. Counselors communicate the parameters of confidentiality in a culturally competent manner.

B.1. Respecting Client Rights

B.1.a. Multicultural/Diversity Considerations

Counselors maintain awareness and sensitivity regarding cultural meanings of confidentiality and privacy. Counselors respect differing views toward disclosure of information. Counselors hold ongoing discussions with clients as to how, when, and with whom information is to be shared.

B.1.b. Respect for Privacy

Counselors respect the privacy of prospective and current clients. Counselors request private information from clients only when it is beneficial to the counseling process.

B.1.a. Respect for Confidentiality

Counselors protect the confidential information of prospective and current clients. Counselors disclose information only with appropriate consent or with sound legal or ethical justification.

B.1.b. Explanation of Limitations

At initiation and throughout the counseling process, counselors inform clients of the limitations of confidentiality and seek to identify situations in which confidentiality must be breached.

B.2. Exceptions

B.2.a. Serious and Foreseeable Harm and Legal Requirements

The general requirement that counselors keep information confidential does not apply when disclosure is required to protect clients or identifying others from serious and foreseeable harm or when legal requirements demand that confidential information must be revealed. Counselors consult with other professionals when in doubt as to the validity of an exception. Additional considerations apply when addressing end-of-life issues.

B.2.b. Confidentiality Regarding End-of-Life Decisions

Counselors who provide services to terminally ill individuals who are considering hastening their own deaths have the option to maintain confidentiality, depending on applicable laws and the specific circumstances of the situation and after seeking consultation or supervision from appropriate professional and legal parties.

B.2.c. Contagious, Life-Threatening Diseases

When clients disclose that they have a disease commonly known to be both communicable and life threatening, counselors may be justified in disclosing information to identified third parties, if the parties are known to be at serious and foreseeable risk of contracting the disease. Prior to making a disclosure, counselors assess the intent of clients to inform the third parties about their disease or to engage in any behaviors that may be harmful to an identified third party. Counselors adhere to relevant state laws concerning disclosure about disease status.

B.2.d Court-Ordered Disclosure

When ordered by a court to release confidential or privileged information without a client's permission, counselors seek to obtain written, informed consent from the client or take steps to prohibit the disclosure or have it limited as narrowly as possible because of potential harm to the client or counseling relationship.

B.2.e. Minimal Disclosure

To the extent possible, clients are informed before confidential information is disclosed and are involved in the disclosure decision-making process. When circumstances require the disclosure of confidential information, only essential information is revealed.

B.3. Information Shared With Others

B.3.a. Subordinates

Counselors make every effort to ensure that privacy and confidentiality of clients are maintained by subordinates, including employees, supervisees, students, clerical assistants, and volunteers.

B.3.b. Interdisciplinary Teams

When services provided to the client involve participation by an interdisciplinary or treatment team, the client will be informed of the team's existence and composition, information being shared, and the purposes of sharing such information.

B.3.c. Confidential Settings

Counselors discuss confidential information only in settings in which they can reasonably ensure client privacy.

B.3.d. Third-Party Payers

Counselors disclose information to third-party payers only when clients have authorized such disclosure.

B.3.e. Transmitting Confidential Information

Counselors take precautions to ensure the confidentiality of all information transmitted through the use of any medium.

B.3.f. Deceased Clients

Counselors protect the confidentiality of deceased clients, consistent with legal requirements and the documented preferences of the client.

B.4. Groups and Families

B.4.a. Group Work

In group work, counselors clearly explain the importance and parameters of confidentiality for the specific group.

B.4.b. Couples and Family Counseling

In couples and family counseling, counselors clearly define who is considered "the client" and discuss expectations and limitations of confidentiality. Counselors seek agreement and document in writing such agreement among all involved parties regarding the confidentiality of information. In the absence of an agreement to the contrary, the couple or family is considered to be the client.

B.5. Clients Lacking Capacity to Give Informed Consent

B.5.a. Responsibility to Clients

When counseling minor clients or adult clients who lack the capacity to give voluntary, informed consent, counselors protect the confidentiality of information received—in any medium—in the counseling relationship as specified by federal and state laws, written policies, and applicable ethical standards.

B.5.b. Responsibility to Parents and Legal Guardians

Counselors inform parents and legal guardians about the role of counselors and the confidential nature of the counseling relationship, consistent with current legal and custodial arrangements. Counselors are sensitive to the cultural diversity of families and respect the inherent rights and responsibilities of parents/guardians regarding the welfare of their children/charges according to law. Counselors work to establish, as appropriate, collaborative relation- ships with parents/guardians to best serve clients.

B.5.c. Release of Confidential Information

When counseling minor clients or adult clients who lack the capacity to give voluntary consent to release confidential information, counselors seek permission from an appropriate third party to disclose information. In such instances, counselors inform clients consistent with their level of understanding and take appropriate measures to of the consultation, and every effort is made to protect client identity and to avoid undue invasion of privacy.

B.6. Records and Documentation

B.6.a. Creating and Maintaining Records and Documentation

Counselors create and maintain records and documentation necessary for rendering professional services.

Section C

Professional Responsibility

Introduction

Counselors aspire to open, honest, and accurate communication in dealing with the public and other professionals. Counselors facilitate access to counseling services, and they practice in a nondiscriminatory manner within the boundaries of professional and personal competence; they also have a responsibility to abide by the *ACA Code of Ethics*. Counselors actively participate in local, state, and national associations that foster the development and improvement of counseling. Counselors are expected to advocate to promote changes at the individual, group, institutional, and societal levels that improve the quality of life for individuals and groups and remove potential barriers to the provision or access of appropriate services being offered. Counselors have a responsibility to the public to engage in counseling practices that are based on rigorous research methodologies. Counselors are encouraged to contribute to society by devoting a portion of their professional activity to services for which there is little or no fi return (*pro bono publico*). In addition, counselors engage in self-care activities to maintain and promote their own emotional, physical, mental, and spiritual well-being to best meet their professional responsibilities.

C.1. Knowledge of and Compliance With Standards

Counselors have a responsibility to read, understand, and follow the *ACA Code of Ethics* and adhere to applicable laws and regulations.

C.2. Professional Competence

C.2.a. Boundaries of Competence

Counselors practice only within the boundaries of their competence, based on their education, training, super- vised experience, state and national professional credentials, and appropriate professional experience. Whereas multicultural counseling competency is required across all counseling specialties, counselors gain knowledge, personal awareness, sensitivity, dispositions, and skills pertinent to being a culturally competent counselor in working with a diverse client population.

C.2.b. New Specialty Areas of Practice

Counselors practice in specialty areas new to them only after appropriate education, training, and supervised experience. While developing skills in new specialty areas, counselors take steps to ensure the competence of their work and protect others from possible harm.

C.2.c. Qualified for Employment

Counselors accept employment only for positions for which they are qualified given their education, training, supervised experience, state and national professional credentials, and appropriate professional experience. Counselors hire for professional counseling positions only individuals who are qualified and competent for those positions.

C.2.d. Monitor Effectiveness

Counselors continually monitor their effectiveness as professionals and take steps to improve when necessary. Counselors take reasonable steps to seek peer supervision to evaluate their effectiveness as counselors.

C.2.e. Consultations on Ethical Obligations

Counselors take reasonable steps to consult with other counselors, the ACA Ethics and Professional Standards Department, or related professionals when they have questions regarding their ethical obligations or professional practice.

C.2.f. Continuing Education

Counselors recognize the need for continuing education to acquire and maintain a reasonable level of awareness of current scientific and professional information in their fields of activity. Counselors maintain their competence in the skills they use, are open to new procedures, and remain informed regarding best practices for working with diverse populations.

C.2.g. Impairment

Counselors monitor themselves for signs of impairment from their own physical, mental, or emotional problems and refrain from offering or providing professional services when impaired. They seek assistance for problems that reach the level of professional impairment, and, if necessary, they limit, suspend, or terminate their professional responsibilities until it is determined that they may safely resume their work. Counselors assist colleagues or supervisors in recognizing their own professional impairment and provide consultation and assistance when war- ranted with colleagues or supervisors showing signs of impairment and intervene as appropriate to prevent imminent harm to clients.

C.2.h. Counselor Incapacitation, Death, Retirement, or Termination of Practice

Counselors prepare a plan for the transfer of clients and the dissemination of records to an identified colleague or records custodian in the case of the counselor's incapacitation, death, retirement, or termination of practice.

C.3. Advertising and Soliciting Clients

C.3.a. Accurate Advertising

When advertising or otherwise rep- resenting their services to the public, counselors identify their credentials in an accurate manner that is not false, misleading, deceptive, or fraudulent.

C.3.b. Testimonials

Counselors who use testimonials do not solicit them from current clients, former clients, or any other persons who may be vulnerable to undue influence. Counselors discuss with clients the implications of and obtain permission for the use of any testimonial.

C.3.c. Statements by Others

When feasible, counselors make reason- able efforts to ensure that statements made by others about them or about the counseling profession are accurate.

C.3.d. Recruiting Through Employment

Counselors do not use their places of employment or institutional affiliation to recruit clients, supervisors, or consultees for their private practices.

C.3.e. Products and Training Advertisements

Counselors who develop products related to their profession or conduct workshops or training events ensure that the advertisements concerning these products or events are accurate and disclose adequate information for consumers to make informed choices.

C.3.f. Promoting to Those Served

Counselors do not use counseling, teaching, training, or supervisory relationships to promote their products or training events in a manner that is deceptive or would exert undue influence on individuals who may be vulnerable. However, counselor educators may adopt textbooks they have authored for instructional purposes.

C.4. Professional Qualification

C.4.a. Accurate Representation

Counselors claim or imply only professional qualification actually completed and correct any known misrepresentations of their qualifications by others. Counselors truthfully represent the qualifications of their professional colleagues. Counselors clearly distinguish between paid and volunteer work experience and accurately describe their continuing education and specialized training.

C.4.b. Credentials

Counselors claim only licenses or certifications that are current and in good standing.

C.4.c. Educational Degrees

Counselors clearly differentiate between earned and honorary degrees.

C.4.d. Implying Doctoral-Level Competence

Counselors clearly state their highest earned degree in counseling or a closely related field. Counselors do not imply doctoral-level competence when possessing a master's degree in counseling or a related field by referring to themselves as "Dr." in a counseling context when their doctorate is not in counseling or a related field. Counselors do not use "ABD" (all but dissertation) or other such terms to imply competency.

Accreditation Status

Counselors accurately represent the accreditation status of their degree program and college/university.

C.4.f. Professional Membership

Counselors clearly differentiate between current, active memberships and former memberships in associations. Members of ACA must clearly differentiate be- tween professional membership, which implies the possession of at least a master's degree in counseling, and regular membership, which is open to individuals whose interests and activities are consistent with those of ACA but are not qualified for professional membership.

C.5. Nondiscrimination

Counselors do not condone or engage in discrimination against prospective or current clients, students, employees, supervisees, or research participants based on age, culture, disability, ethnicity, race, religion/spirituality, gender, gender identity, sexual orientation, marital/ partnership status, language preference, socioeconomic status, immigration status, or any basis proscribed by law.

C.6. Public Responsibility

C.6.a. Sexual Harassment
Counselors do not engage in or condone sexual harassment. Sexual harassment can consist of a single intense or severe act, or multiple persistent or pervasive acts.

C.6.b. Reports to Third Parties Counselors are accurate, honest, and objective in reporting their professional activities and judgments to appropriate third parties, including courts, health insurance companies, those who are the recipients of evaluation reports, and others.

C.6.c. Media Presentations

When counselors provide advice or comment by means of public lectures, demonstrations, radio or television programs, recordings, technology-based applications, printed articles, mailed material, or other media, they take reasonable precautions to ensure that

1. the statements are based on appropriate professional counseling literature and practice,
2. the statements are otherwise consistent with the *ACA Code of Ethics*, and
3. the recipients of the information are not encouraged to infer that a professional counseling relation- ship has been established

C.6.d. Exploitation of Others
Counselors do not exploit others in their professional relationships.

C.6.e. Contributing to the Public Good

(Pro Bono Publico)
Counselors make a reasonable effort to provide services to the public for which there is little or no financial return (e.g., speaking to groups, sharing professional information, offering reduced fees).

C.7. Treatment Modalities

C.7.a. Scientific Basis for Treatment

When providing services, counselors use techniques/procedures/ modalities that are grounded in theory and/or have an empirical or scientific foundation.

C.7.b. Development and Innovation

When counselors use developing or innovative techniques /procedures/ modalities, they explain the potential risks, benefits and ethical considerations of using such techniques/procedures/ modalities. Counselors work to minimize any potential risks or harm when using these techniques/procedures/modalities.

C.7.c. Harmful Practices
Counselors do not use techniques/procedures/modalities when substantial evidence suggests harm, even if such services are requested.

C.8. Responsibility to Other Professionals

C.8.a. Personal Public Statements

When making personal statements in a public context, counselors clarify that they are speaking from their personal perspectives and that they are not speaking on behalf of all counselors or the profession.

Section D
Relationships With Other Professionals

Introduction
Professional counselors recognize that the quality of their interactions with colleagues can influence the quality of services provided to clients. They work to become knowledgeable about colleagues within and outside the field of counseling. Counselors develop positive working relation- ships and systems of communication with colleagues to enhance services to clients.

D.1. Relationships With Colleagues, Employers, and Employees

D.1.a. Different Approaches
Counselors are respectful of approaches that are grounded in theory and/or have an empirical or scientific foundation but may differ from their own. Counselors acknowledge the expertise of other professional groups and are respectful of their practices.

D.1.b. Forming Relationships

Counselors work to develop and strengthen relationships with col- leagues from other disciplines to best serve clients.

D.1.c. Interdisciplinary Teamwork

Counselors who are members of interdisciplinary teams delivering multifaceted services to clients remain focused on how to best serve clients. They participate in and contribute to decisions that affect the well-being of clients by drawing on the perspectives, values, and experiences of the counseling profession and those of colleagues from other disciplines.

D.1.d. Establishing Professional and Ethical Obligations

Counselors who are members of inter-disciplinary teams work together with team members to clarify professional and ethical obligations of the team as a whole and of its individual members. When a team decision raises ethical concerns, counselors fi attempt to resolve the concern within the team. If they cannot reach resolution among team members, counselors pursue other avenues to address their concerns consistent with client well-being.

D.1.e. Confidentiality

When counselors are required by law, institutional policy, or extraordinary circumstances to serve in more than one role in judicial or administrative proceedings, they clarify role expectations and the parameters of confidentiality with their colleagues.

D.1.f. Personnel Selection and Assignment

When counselors are in a position requiring personnel selection and/or assigning of responsibilities to others, they select competent staff and assign responsibilities compatible with their skills and experiences.

D.1.g. Employer Policies

The acceptance of employment in an agency or institution implies that counselors are in agreement with its general policies and principles. Counselors strive to reach agreement with employers regarding acceptable standards of client care and professional conduct that allow for changes in institutional policy conducive to the growth and development of clients.

D.1.h. Negative Conditions

Counselors alert their employers of inappropriate policies and practices. They attempt to effect changes in such policies or procedures through constructive action within the organization. When such policies are potentially disruptive or damaging to clients or may limit the effectiveness of services provided and change cannot be affected, counselors take appropriate further action. Such action may include referral to appropriate certifications, accreditation, or state licensure organizations, or voluntary termination of employment.

D.1.i. Protection From Punitive Action

Counselors do not harass a colleague or employee or dismiss an employee who has acted in a responsible and ethical manner to expose inappropriate employer policies or practices.

D.2. Provision of Consultation Services

D.2.a. Consultant Competency

Counselors take reasonable steps to ensure that they have the appropriate resources and competencies when providing consultation services. Counselors provide appropriate referral resources when requested or needed.

D.2.b. Informed Consent in Formal Consultation

When providing formal consultation services, counselors have an obligation to review, in writing and verbally, the rights and responsibilities of both counselors and consultees. Counselors use clear and understandable language to inform all parties involved about the purpose of the services to be provided, relevant costs, potential risks and benefits, and the limits of confidentiality.

Section E
Evaluation, Assessment, and Interpretation

Introduction

Counselors use assessment as one component of the counseling process, taking into account the clients' personal and cultural context. Counselors promote the well-being of individual clients or groups of clients by developing and using appropriate educational, mental health, psychological, and career assessments.

E.1. General

E.1.a. Assessment

The primary purpose of educational, mental health, psychological, and career assessment is to gather information regarding the client for a variety of purposes, including, but not limited to, client decision making, treatment planning, and forensic proceedings. Assessment may include both qualitative and quantitative methodologies.

E.1.b. Client Welfare

Counselors do not misuse assessment results and interpretations, and they take reasonable steps to prevent others from misusing the information pro- vided. They respect the client's right to know the results, the interpretations made, and the bases for counselors' conclusions and recommendations.

E.2. Competence to Use and Interpret Assessment Instruments

E.2.a. Limits of Competence

Counselors use only those testing and assessment services for which they have been trained and are competent. Counselors using technology-assisted test interpretations are trained in the construct being measured and the specific instrument being used prior to using its technology-based application. Counselors take reasonable measures to ensure the proper use of assessment techniques by persons under their supervision.

E.2.b. Appropriate Use

Counselors are responsible for the appropriate application, scoring, interpretation, and use of assessment instruments relevant to the needs of the client, whether they score and interpret such assessments themselves or use technology or other services.

E.2.c. Decisions Based on Results

Counselors responsible for decisions involving individuals or policies that are based on assessment results have a thorough understanding of psychometrics.

E.3. Informed Consent in Assessment

E.3.a. Explanation to Clients
Prior to assessment, counselors explain the nature and purposes of assessment and the specific use of results by potential recipients. The explanation will be given in terms and language that the client (or other legally authorized person on behalf of the client) can understand.

E.3.b. Recipients of Results
Counselors consider the client's and/or examinee's welfare, explicit under-standings, and prior agreements in determining who receives the assessment results. Counselors include accurate and appropriate interpretations with any release of individual or group assessment results.

E.4. Release of Data to Qualified Personnel

Counselors release assessment data in which the client is identified only with the consent of the client or the client's legal representative. Such data are released only to persons recognized by counselors as qualified to interpret the data.

E.5. Diagnosis of Mental Disorders

E.5.a. Proper Diagnosis
Counselors take special care to provide proper diagnosis of mental disorders. Assessment techniques (including personal interviews) used to determine client care (e.g., locus of treatment, type of treatment, recommended follow-up) are carefully selected and appropriately used.

E.5.b. Cultural Sensitivity

Counselors recognize that culture affects the manner in which clients' problems are defined and experienced. Clients' socioeconomic and cultural experiences are considered when diagnosing mental disorders.

E.5.c. Historical and Social Prejudices in the Diagnosis of Pathology

Counselors recognize historical and social prejudices in the misdiagnosis and pathologizing of certain individuals and groups and strive to become aware of and address such biases in themselves or others.

E.5.d. Refraining From Diagnosis

Counselors may refrain from making and/or reporting a diagnosis if they believe that it would cause harm to the client or others. Counselors carefully consider both the positive and negative implications of a diagnosis.

E.6. Instrument Selection

E.6.a. Appropriateness of Instruments

Counselors carefully consider the validity, reliability, psychometric limitations, and appropriateness of instruments when selecting assessments and, when possible, use multiple forms of assessment, data, and/or instruments in forming conclusions, diagnoses, or recommendations.

E.6.b. Referral Information

If a client is referred to a third party for assessment, the counselor provides specific referral questions and sufficient objective data about the client to ensure that appropriate assessment instruments are utilized.

E.7. Conditions of Assessment Administration

E.7.a. Administration Conditions

Counselors administer assessments under the same conditions that were established in their standardization. When assessments are not administered under standard conditions, as may be necessary to accommodate clients with disabilities, or when unusual behavior or irregularities occur during the administration, those conditions are noted in interpretation, and the results may be designated as invalid or of question-able validity.

E.7.b. Provision of Favorable Conditions

Counselors provide an appropriate environment for the administration of assessments (e.g., privacy, comfort, freedom from distraction).

E.7.c. Technological Administration

Counselors ensure that technologically administered assessments function properly and provide clients with accurate results.

E.7.d. Unsupervised Assessments

Unless the assessment instrument is designed, intended, and validated for self-administration and/or scoring, counselors do not permit unsupervised use.

E.8. Multicultural Issues/Diversity in Assessment

Counselors select and use with caution assessment techniques normed on populations other than that of the client. Counselors recognize the effects of age, color, culture, disability, ethnic group, gender, race, language preference, religion, spirituality, sexual orientation, and socioeconomic status on test administration and interpretation, and they place test results in proper perspective with other relevant factors.

E.9. Scoring and Interpretation of Assessments

E.9.a. Reporting

When counselors report assessment results, they consider the client's personal and cultural background, the level of the client's understanding of the results, and the impact of the results on the client. In reporting assessment results, counselors indicate reservations that exist regarding validity or reliability due to circumstances of the assessment or inappropriateness of the norms for the person tested.

E.9.b. Instruments With Insufficient Empirical Data

Counselors exercise caution when interpreting the results of instruments not having sufficient empirical data to support respondent results. The specific purposes for the use of such instruments are stated explicitly to the examinee. Counselors qualify any conclusions, diagnoses, or recommendations made that are based on assessments or instruments with questionable validity or reliability.

E.9.c. Assessment Services

Counselors who provide assessment, scoring, and interpretation services to support the assessment process confirm the validity of such interpretations. They accurately describe the purpose, norms, validity, reliability, and applications of the procedures and any special qualification applicable to their use. At all times, counselors maintain their ethical responsibility to those being assessed.

E.10. Assessment Security

Counselors maintain the integrity and security of tests and assessments consistent with legal and contractual obligations. Counselors do not appropriate, reproduce, or modify published assessments or parts thereof without acknowledgment and permission from the publisher.

E.11. Obsolete Assessment and Outdated Results

Counselors do not use data or results from assessments that are obsolete or outdated for the current purpose (e.g., noncurrent versions of assessments/ instruments). Counselors make every effort to prevent the misuse of obsolete measures and assessment data by others.

E.12. Assessment Construction

Counselors use established scientific procedures, relevant standards, and current professional knowledge for assessment design in the development, publication, and utilization of assessment techniques.

E.13. Forensic Evaluation: Evaluation for Legal Proceedings

E.13.a. Primary Obligations

When providing forensic evaluations, the primary obligation of counselors is to produce objective findings that can be substantiated based on information and techniques appropriate to the evaluation, which may include examination of the individual and/or review of records. Counselors form professional opinions based on their professional knowledge and expertise that can be supported by the data gathered in evaluations. Counselors define the limits of their reports or testimony, especially when an examination of the individual has not been conducted.

E.13.b. Consent for Evaluation

Individuals being evaluated are in- formed in writing that the relationship is for the purposes of an evaluation and is not therapeutic in nature, and entities or individuals who will receive the evaluation report are identified. Counselors who perform forensic evaluations obtain written consent from those being evaluated or from their legal representative unless a court orders evaluations to be conducted without the written consent of the individuals being evaluated. When children or adults who lack the capacity to give voluntary consent are being evaluated, informed written consent is obtained from a parent or guardian.

E.13.c. Client Evaluation Prohibited

Counselors do not evaluate current or former clients, clients' romantic partners, or clients' family members for forensic purposes. Counselors do not counsel individuals they are evaluating.

E.13.d. Avoid Potentially Harmful Relationships

Counselors who provide forensic evaluations avoid potentially harmful professional or personal relationships with family members, romantic partners, and close friends of individuals they are evaluating or have evaluated in the past.

Section F
Supervision, Training, and Teaching

Introduction

Counselor supervisors, trainers, and educators aspire to foster meaningful and respectful professional relation- ships and to maintain appropriate boundaries with supervisees and students in both face-to-face and electronic formats. They have theoretical and pedagogical foundations for their work; have knowledge of supervision models; and aim to be fair, accurate, and honest in their assessments of counselors, students, and supervisees.

F.1. Counselor Supervision and Client Welfare

F.1.a. Client Welfare

A primary obligation of counseling supervisors is to monitor the services provided by supervisees. Counseling supervisors monitor client welfare and supervisee performance and professional development. To fulfill these obligations, supervisors meet regularly with supervisees to review the supervisees' work and help them become prepared to serve a range of diverse clients. Supervisees have a responsibility to understand and follow the *ACA Code of Ethics*.

F.1.b. Client Welfare Counselor Credentials

Counseling supervisors work to ensure that supervisees communicate their qualifications to render services to their clients.

F.1.c. Informed Consent and Client Rights

Supervisors make supervisees aware of client rights, including the protection of client privacy and confidentiality in the counseling relationship. Supervisees provide clients with professional disclosure information and inform them of how the supervision process influences the limits of confidentiality. Supervisees make clients aware of who will have access to records of the counseling relationship and how these records will be stored, transmitted, or otherwise reviewed.

F.2. Counselor Supervision Competence

F.2.a. Supervisor Preparation

Prior to offering supervision services, counselors are trained in supervision methods and techniques. Counselors who offer supervision services regularly pursue continuing education activities, including both counseling and supervision topics and skills.

F.2.b. Multicultural Issues/Diversity in Supervision

Counseling supervisors are aware of and address the role of multiculturalism/ diversity in the supervisory relationship.

F.2.c. Online Supervision

When using technology in supervision, counselor supervisors are competent in the use of those technologies. Supervisors take the necessary precautions to protect the confidentiality of all information transmitted through any electronic means.

F.3. Supervisory Relationship

F.3.a. Extending Conventional Supervisory Relationships

Counseling supervisors clearly define and maintain ethical professional, personal, and social relationships with their supervisees. Supervisors con- sider the risks and benefit of extending current supervisory relationships in any form beyond conventional parameters. In extending these boundaries, supervisors take appropriate professional precautions to ensure that judgment is not impaired and that no harm occurs.

F.3.b. Sexual Relationships

Sexual or romantic interactions or relationships with current supervisees are prohibited. This prohibition applies to both in-person and electronic interactions or relationships.

F.3.c. Sexual Harassment

Counseling supervisors do not con- done or subject supervisees to sexual harassment.

F.3.d. Friends or Family Members

Supervisors are prohibited from engaging in supervisory relationships with individuals with whom they have an inability to remain objective.

F.4. Supervisor Responsibilities

F.4.a. Informed Consent for Supervision

Supervisors are responsible for incorporating into their supervision the principles of informed consent and participation. Supervisors inform supervisees of the policies and procedures to which supervisors are to adhere and the mechanisms for due process appeal of individual supervisor actions. The issues unique to the use of distance supervision are to be included in the documentation as necessary.

F.4.b. Emergencies and Absences

Supervisors establish and communicate to supervisees procedures for contacting supervisors or, in their absence, alternative on-call supervisors to assist in handling crises.

F.4.c. Standards for Supervisees

Supervisors make their supervisees aware of professional and ethical standards and legal responsibilities.

F.4.d. Termination of the Supervisory Relationship

Supervisors or supervisees have the right to terminate the supervisory relationship with adequate notice. Rea- sons for considering termination are discussed, and both parties work to resolve differences. When termination is warranted, supervisors make appropriate referrals to possible alternative supervisors.

F.5. Student and Supervisee Responsibilities

F.5.a. Ethical Responsibilities
Students and supervisees have a responsibility to understand and follow the *ACA Code of Ethics*. Students and supervisees have the same obligation to clients as those required of professional counselors.

F.5.b. Impairment
Students and supervisees monitor themselves for signs of impairment from their own physical, mental, or emotional problems and refrain from offering or providing professional services when such impairment is likely to harm a client or others. They notify their faculty and/or supervisors and seek assistance for problems that reach the level of professional impairment, and, if necessary, they limit, suspend, or terminate their professional responsibilities until it is determined that they may safely resume their work.

F.5.c. Professional Disclosure
Before providing counseling services, students and supervisees disclose their status as supervisees and explain how this status affects the limits of confidentiality. Supervisors ensure that clients are aware of the services rendered and the qualifications of the students and supervisees rendering those services. Students and supervisees obtain client permission before they use any information concerning the counseling relationship in the training process.

F.6. Counseling Supervision Evaluation, Remediation, and Endorsement

F.6.a. Evaluation
Supervisors document and provide supervisees with ongoing feedback regarding their performance and schedule periodic formal evaluative sessions throughout the supervisory relationship.

F.6.b. Gatekeeping and Remediation
Through initial and ongoing evaluation, supervisors are aware of supervisee limitations that might impede performance. Supervisors assist supervisees in securing remedial assistance when needed. They recommend dismissal from training programs, applied counseling settings, and state or voluntary professional credentialing processes when those supervisees are unable to demonstrate that they can provide competent professional services to a range of diverse clients. Supervisors seek consultation and document their decisions to dismiss or refer supervisees for assistance. They ensure that supervisees are aware of options available to them to address such decisions.

F.6.c. Counseling for Supervisees
If supervisees request counseling, the supervisor assists the supervisee in identifying appropriate services. Supervisors do not provide counseling services to supervisees. Supervisors address interpersonal competencies in terms of the impact of these issues on clients, the supervisory relationship, and professional functioning.

F.6.d. Endorsements
Supervisors endorse supervisees for certification, licensure, employment, or completion of an academic or training program only when they believe that supervisees are qualified for the endorsement. Regardless of qualifications, supervisors do not endorse supervisees whom they believe to be impaired in any way that would interfere with the performance of the duties associated with the endorsement.

F.7. Responsibilities of Counselor Educators

F.7.a. Counselor Educators
Counselor educators who are responsible for developing, implementing, and supervising educational programs are skilled as teachers and practitioners. They are knowledgeable regarding regulatory aspects of the profession; are skilled in applying that knowledge; and make students and supervisees aware of their responsibilities. Whether in traditional, hybrid, and/or online formats, counselor educators conduct counselor education and training programs in an ethical manner and serve as role models for professional behavior.

F.7.b. Counselor Educator Competence
Counselors who function as counselor educators or supervisors provide instruction within their areas of knowledge and competence and provide instruction based on current information and knowledge available in the profession. When using technology to deliver instruction, counselor educators develop competence in the use of the technology.

F.7.c. Infusing Multicultural Issues/Diversity
Counselor educators infuse material related to multiculturalism/diversity into all courses and workshops for the development of professional counselors.

F.7.d. Integration of Study and Practice
In traditional, hybrid, and/or online formats, counselor educators establish education and training programs that integrate academic study and super- vised practice.

F.7.e. Teaching Ethics
Throughout the program, counselor educators ensure that students are aware of the ethical responsibilities and standards of the profession and the ethical responsibilities of students to the profession. Counselor educators

infuse ethical considerations throughout the curriculum.

F.7.f. Use of Case Examples

The use of client, student, or supervisee information for the purposes of case examples in a lecture or classroom setting is permissible only when (a) the client, student, or supervisee has reviewed the material and agreed to its presentation or (b) the information has been sufficiently modified to obscure identity.

F.7.g. Student-to-Student Supervision and Instruction

When students function in the role of counselor educators or supervisors, they understand that they have the same ethical obligations as counselor educators, trainers, and supervisors. Counselor educators make every effort to ensure that the rights of students are not compromised when their peers lead experiential counseling activities in traditional, hybrid, and/or online formats (e.g., counseling groups, skills classes, clinical supervision).

F.7.h. Innovative Theories and Techniques

Counselor educators promote the use of techniques/procedures/modalities that are grounded in theory and/or have an empirical or scientific foundation. When counselor educators discuss developing or innovative techniques/ procedures/modalities, they explain the potential risks, benefits, and ethical considerations of using such techniques/ procedures/modalities.

F.7.i. Field Placements

Counselor educators develop clear policies and provide direct assistance within their training programs regarding appropriate field placement and other clinical experiences. Counselor educators provide clearly stated roles and responsibilities for the student or supervisee, the site supervisor, and the program supervisor. They confirm that site supervisors are qualified to provide supervision in the formats in which services are provided and inform site supervisors of their professional and ethical responsibilities in this role.

F.8. Student Welfare

F.8.a. Program Information and Orientation

Counselor educators recognize that program orientation is a developmental process that begins upon students' initial contact with the counselor education program and continues throughout the educational and clinical training of students. Counselor education faculty provide prospective and current students with information about the counselor education program's expectations, including

1. the values and ethical principles of the profession;
2. the type and level of skill and knowledge acquisition required for successful completion of the training;
3. technology requirements;
4. program training goals, objectives, and mission, and subject matter to be covered;
5. bases for evaluation;
6. training components that encourage self-growth or self-disclosure as part of the training process;
7. the type of supervision settings and requirements of the sites for required clinical field experiences;
8. student and supervisor evaluation and dismissal policies and procedures; and
9. up-to-date employment prospects for graduates.

F.8.b. Student Career Advising

Counselor educators provide career advisement for their students and make them aware of opportunities in the field.

F.8.c. Self-Growth Experiences

Self-growth is an expected component of counselor education. Counselor educators are mindful of ethical principles when they require students to engage in self-growth experiences. Counselor educators and supervisors inform students that they have a right to decide what information will be shared or withheld in class.

F.8.d. Addressing Personal Concerns

Counselor educators may require students to address any personal concerns that have the potential to affect professional competency.

F.9. Evaluation and Remediation

F.9.a. Evaluation of Students

Counselor educators clearly state to students, prior to and throughout the training program, the levels of competency expected, appraisal methods, and timing of evaluations for both didactic and clinical competencies. Counselor educators provide students with ongoing feedback regarding their performance throughout the training program.

F.9.b. Limitations

Counselor educators, through ongoing evaluation, are aware of and address the inability of some students to achieve counseling competencies. Counselor educators do the following:

1. assist students in securing remedial assistance when needed,
2. seek professional consultation and document their decision to dismiss or refer students for assistance, and
3. ensure that students have recourse in a timely manner to address decisions requiring them to seek assistance or to dismiss them and provide students with due process according to institutional policies and procedures.

F.9.c. Counseling for Students

If students request counseling, or if counseling services are suggested as part of a remediation process, counselor educators assist students in identifying appropriate services.

F.10. Roles and Relationships Between Counselor Educators and Students

F.10.a. Sexual or Romantic Relationships

Counselor educators are prohibited from sexual or romantic interactions or relationships with students currently enrolled in a counseling or related program and over whom they have power and authority. This prohibition applies to both in-person and electronic interactions or relationships.

F.10.b. Sexual Harassment

Counselor educators do not condone or subject students to sexual harassment.

F.10.c. Relationships With Former Students

Counselor educators are aware of the power differential in the relationship between faculty and students. Faculty members discuss with former students potential risks when they consider engaging in social, sexual, or other intimate relationships.

F.10.d. Nonacademic Relationships

Counselor educators avoid nonacademic relationships with students in which there is a risk of potential harm to the student or which may compromise the training experience or grades assigned. In addition, counselor educators do not accept any form of professional services, fees, commissions, reimbursement, or remuneration from a site for student or supervisor placement.

F.10.e. Counseling Services

Counselor educators do not serve as counselors to students currently enrolled in a counseling or related program and over whom they have power and authority.

F.10.f. Extending Educator–Student Boundaries

Counselor educators are aware of the power differential in the relationship between faculty and students. If they believe that a nonprofessional relationship with a student may be potentially beneficial to the student, they take precautions similar to those taken by counselors when working with clients. Examples of potentially beneficial interactions or relationships include, but are not limited to, attending a formal ceremony; conducting hospital visits; providing support during a stressful event; or maintaining mutual membership in a professional association, organization, or community. Counselor educators discuss with students the rationale for such interactions, the potential benefits and drawbacks, and the anticipated consequences for the student. Educators clarify the specific nature and limitations of the additional role(s) they will have with the student prior to engaging in a nonprofessional relationship. Nonprofessional relationships with students should be time limited and/or context specific and initiated with student consent.

F.11. Multicultural/Diversity Competence in Counselor Education and Training Programs

F.11.a. Faculty Diversity

Counselor educators are committed to recruiting and retaining a diverse faculty.

F.11.b. Student Diversity

Counselor educators actively attempt to recruit and retain a diverse student body. Counselor educators demonstrate commitment to multicultural /diversity competence by recognizing and valuing the diverse cultures and types of abilities that students bring to the training experience. Counselor educators provide appropriate accommodations that enhance and support diverse student well-being and academic performance

F.11.c. Multicultural/ Diversity Competence

Counselor educators actively infuse multicultural/diversity competency in their training and supervision practices. They actively train students to gain awareness, knowledge, and skills in the competencies of multicultural practice.

Section G

Research and Publication

Introduction

Counselors who conduct research are encouraged to contribute to the knowledge base of the profession and promote a clearer understanding of the conditions that lead to a healthy and more just society. Counselors support the efforts of researchers by participating fully and willingly whenever possible. Counselors minimize bias and respect diversity in designing and implementing research.

G.1. Research Responsibilities

G.1.a. Conducting Research

Counselors plan, design, conduct, and report research in a manner that is consistent with pertinent ethical principles, federal and state laws, host institutional regulations, and scientific standards governing research.

G.1.b. Confidentiality in Research

Counselors are responsible for understanding and adhering to state, federal, agency, or institutional policies or applicable guidelines regarding confidentiality in their research practices.

G.1.c. Independent Researcher

When counselors conduct independent research and do not have access to an institutional review board, they are bound to the same ethical principles and federal and state laws pertaining to the review of their plan, design, conduct, and reporting of research.

G.1.d. Deviation From Standard Practice

Counselors seek consultation and observe stringent safeguards to protect the rights of research participants when research indicates that a deviation from standard or acceptable practices may be necessary.

G.1.e. Precautions to Avoid Injury

Counselors who conduct research are responsible for their participants' welfare throughout the research process and should take reasonable precautions to avoid causing emotional, physical, or social harm to participants.

G.1.f. Principal Researcher Responsibility

The ultimate responsibility for ethical research practice lies with the principal researcher. All others involved in the re- search activities share ethical obligations and responsibility for their own actions.

G.2. Rights of Research Participants

G.2.a. Informed Consent in Research

Individuals have the right to decline requests to become research participants. In seeking consent, counselors use language that

1. accurately explains the purpose and procedures to be followed;
2. identifies any procedures that are experimental or relatively untried;
3. describes any attendant discomforts, risks, and potential power differentials between researchers and participants;
4. describes any benefits or changes in individuals or organizations that might reasonably be expected;
5. discloses appropriate alternative procedures that would be advantageous for participants;
6. offers to answer any inquiries concerning the procedures;
7. describes any limitations on confidentiality;
8. describes the format and potential target audiences for the dissemination of research finances and
9. instructs participants that they are free to withdraw their consent and discontinue participation in the project at any time, without penalty.

G.2.b. Student/Supervisee Participation

Researchers who involve students or supervisees in research make clear to them that the decision regarding participation in research activities does not affect their academic standing or supervisory relationship. Students or supervisees who choose not to participate in research are provided with an appropriate alternative to fulfill their academic or clinical requirements.

G.2.c. Client Participation

Counselors conducting research involving clients make clear in the informed consent process that clients are free to choose whether to participate in re- search activities. Counselors take necessary precautions to protect clients from adverse consequences of declining or withdrawing from participation.

G.2.d. Confidentiality of Information

Information obtained about research participants during the course of re- search is confidential Procedures are implemented to protect confidentiality.

G.2.e. Persons Not Capable of Giving Informed Consent

When a research participant is not capable of giving informed consent, counselors provide an appropriate explanation to, obtain agreement for participation from, and obtain the appropriate consent of a legally authorized person.

G.2.f. Commitments to Participants

Counselors take reasonable measures to honor all commitments to research participants.

G.2.g. Explanations After Data Collection

After data are collected, counselors provide participants with full clarification of the nature of the study to re- move any misconceptions participants might have regarding the research. Where scientific or human values justify delaying or withholding information, counselors take reasonable measures to avoid causing harm.

G.2.h. Informing Sponsors

Counselors inform sponsors, institutions, and publication channels regarding research procedures and outcomes. Counselors ensure that appropriate bodies and authorities are given pertinent information and acknowledgment.

G.2.i. Research Records Custodian

As appropriate, researchers prepare and disseminate to an identified colleague or records custodian a plan for the transfer of research data in the case of their incapacitation, retirement, or death.

G.3. Managing and Maintaining Boundaries

G.3.a. Extending Researcher–Participant Boundaries

Researchers consider the risks and benefits of extending current research relationships beyond conventional parameters. When a non-research interaction between the researcher and the research participant may be potentially beneficial, the researcher must document, prior to the interaction (when feasible), the rationale for such an interaction, the potential benefit, and anticipated consequences for the research participant. Such interactions should be initiated with appropriate consent of the research participant. Where unintentional harm occurs to the research participant, the researcher must show evidence of an attempt to remedy such harm.

G.3.b. Relationships With Research Participants

Sexual or romantic counselor–research participant interactions or relationships with current research participants are prohibited. This prohibition applies to both in-person and electronic interactions or relationships.

G.3.c. Sexual Harassment and Research Participants

Researchers do not condone or subject re- search participants to sexual harassment.

G.4. Reporting Results

G.4.a. Accurate Results
Counselors plan, conduct, and report research accurately. Counselors do not engage in misleading or fraudulent research, distort data, misrepresent data, or deliberately bias their results. They describe the extent to which results are applicable for diverse populations.

G.4.b. Obligation to Report Unfavorable Results

Counselors report the results of any research of professional value. Results that reflect unfavorably on institutions, programs, services, prevailing opinions, or vested interests are not withheld.

G.4.c. Reporting Errors

If counselors discover significant errors in their published research, they take reasonable steps to correct such errors in a correction erratum or through other appropriate publication means.

G.4.d. Identity of Participants

Counselors who supply data, aid in the research of another person, report research results, or make original data available take due care to disguise the identity of respective participants in the absence of specific authorization from the participants to do otherwise. In situations where participants self- identify their involvement in research studies, researchers take active steps to ensure that data are adapted/changed to protect the identity and welfare of all parties and that discussion of results does not cause harm to participants.

G.4.e. Replication Studies

Counselors are obligated to make available sufficient original research information to qualified professionals who may wish to replicate or extend the study

G.5. Publications and Presentations

G.5.a. Use of Case Examples

The use of participants', clients', students', or supervisees' information for the purpose of case examples in a presentation or publication is permissible only when (a) participants, clients, students, or supervisees have reviewed the material and agreed to its presentation or publication or (b) the information has been sufficiently modified to obscure identity.

G.5.b. Plagiarism

Counselors do not plagiarize; that is, they do not present another person's work as their own.

G.5.c. Acknowledging Previous Work

In publications and presentations, counselors acknowledge and give recognition to previous work on the topic by others or self.

G.5.d. Contributors

Counselors give credit through joint authorship, acknowledgment, foot- note statements, or other appropriate means to those who have contributed significantly to research or concept development in accordance with such contributions. The principal contributor is listed fi and minor technical or professional contributions are acknowledged in notes or introductory statements.

G.5.e. Agreement of Contributors

Counselors who conduct joint research with colleagues or students/supervisors establish agreements in advance regarding allocation of tasks, publication credit, and types of acknowledgment that will be received.

G.5.f. Student Research

Manuscripts or professional presentations in any medium that are substantially based on a student's course papers, projects, dissertations, or theses are used only with the student's permission and list the student as lead author.

G.5.g. Duplicate Submissions

Counselors submit manuscripts for consideration to only one journal at a time. Manuscripts that are published in whole or in substantial part in one journal or published work are not submitted for publication to another publisher with- out acknowledgment and permission from the original publisher.

G.5.h. Professional Review

Counselors who review material sub- mitted for publication, research, or other scholarly purposes respect the confidentiality and proprietary rights of those who submitted it. Counselors make publication decisions based on valid and defensible standards. Counselors review article submissions in a timely manner and based on their scope and competency in research methodologies. Counselors who serve as reviewers at the request of editors or publishers make every effort to only review materials that are within their scope of competency and avoid personal biases.

Section H

Distance Counseling, Technology, and Social Media

Introduction

Counselors understand that the profession of counseling may no longer be limited to in-person, face-to-face inter- actions. Counselors actively attempt to understand the evolving nature of the profession with regard to distance counseling, technology, and social media and how such resources may be used to better serve their clients. Counselors strive to become knowledgeable about these resources. Counselors understand the additional concerns related to the use of distance counseling, technology, and social media and make every attempt to protect confidentiality and meet any legal and ethical requirements for the use of such resources.

H.1. Knowledge and Legal Considerations

H.1.a. Knowledge and Competency

Counselors who engage in the use of distance counseling, technology, and/ or social media develop knowledge and skills regarding related technical, ethical, and legal considerations (e.g., special certified additional course work).

H.1.b. Laws and Statutes

Counselors who engage in the use of distance counseling, technology, and social media within their counseling practice understand that they may be subject to laws and regulations of both the counselor's practicing location and the client's place of residence. Counselors ensure that their clients are aware of pertinent legal rights and limitations governing the practice of counseling across state lines or international boundaries.

H.2. Informed Consent and Security

H.2.a. Informed Consent and Disclosure

Clients have the freedom to choose whether to use distance counseling, social media, and/or technology within the counseling process. In addition to the usual and customary protocol of informed consent between counselor and client for face-to-face counseling, the following issues, unique to the use of distance counseling, technology, and/ or social media, are addressed in the informed consent process:

- distance counseling credentials, physical location of practice, and contact information;
- risks and benefits of engaging in the use of distance counseling, technology, and/or social media;
- possibility of technology failure and alternate methods of service delivery;
- anticipated response time;
- emergency procedures to follow when the counselor is not available;
- time zone differences;
- cultural and/or language differences that may affect delivery of services;
- possible denial of insurance benefits; and
- social media policy.

H.2.b. Confidentiality Maintained by the Counselor

Counselors acknowledge the limitations of maintaining the confidentiality of electronic records and transmissions. They inform clients that individuals might have authorized or unauthorized access to such records or transmissions (e.g., colleagues, supervisors, employees, information technologists).

H.2.c. Acknowledgment of Limitations

Counselors inform clients about the inherent limits of confidentiality when using technology. Counselors urge clients to be aware of authorized and/ or unauthorized access to information disclosed using this medium in the counseling process.

H.2.d. Security

Counselors use current encryption standards within their websites and/or technology-based communications that meet applicable legal requirements. Counselors take reasonable precautions to ensure the confidentiality of information transmitted through any electronic means.

H.3. Client Verification

Counselors who engage in the use of distance counseling, technology, and/ or social media to interact with clients take steps to verify the client's identity at the beginning and throughout the therapeutic process. Verification can include, but is not limited to, using code words, numbers, graphics, or other nondescript identifiers.

H.4. Distance Counseling Relationship

H.4.a. Benefits and Limitations

Counselors inform clients of the benefits and limitations of using technology applications in the provision of counseling services. Such technologies include, but are not limited to, computer hardware and/or software, telephones and applications, social media and Internet-based applications and other audio and/or video communication, or data storage devices or media.

H.4.b. Professional Boundaries in Distance Counseling

Counselors understand the necessity of maintaining a professional relationship with their clients. Counselors discuss and establish professional boundaries with clients regarding the appropriate use and/or application of technology and the limitations of its use within the counseling relationship (e.g., lack of confidentiality, times when not appropriate to use).

H.4.c. Technology-Assisted Services

When providing technology-assisted services, counselors make reasonable efforts to determine that clients are intellectually, emotionally, physically, linguistically, and functionally capable of using the application and that the application is appropriate for the needs of the client. Counselors verify that clients understand the purpose and operation of technology applications and follow up with clients to correct possible misconceptions, discover appropriate use, and assess subsequent steps.

H.4.d. Effectiveness of Services

When distance counseling services are deemed ineffective by the counselor or client, counselors consider delivering services face-to-face. If the counselor is not able to provide face-to-face services (e.g., lives in another state), the counselor assists the client in identifying appropriate services.

H.4.e. Access

Counselors provide information to clients regarding reasonable access to pertinent applications when providing technology-assisted services.

H.4.f. Communication Differences in Electronic Media

Counselors consider the differences between face-to-face and electronic communication (nonverbal and verbal cues) and how these may affect the counseling process. Counselors educate clients on how to prevent and address potential misunderstandings arising from the lack of visual cues and voice intonations when communicating electronically.

H.5. Records and Web Maintenance

H.5.a. Records

Counselors maintain electronic records in accordance with relevant laws and statutes. Counselors inform clients on how records are maintained electronically. This includes, but is not limited to, the type of encryption and security assigned to the records, and if/for how long archival storage of transaction records is maintained.

H.5.b. Client Rights

Counselors who offer distance counseling services and/or maintain a professional website provide electronic links to relevant licensure and professional certification boards to protect consumer and client rights and address ethical concerns.

H.5.c. Electronic Links

Counselors regularly ensure that electronic links are working and are professionally appropriate.

H.5.d. Multicultural and Disability Considerations

Counselors who maintain websites provide accessibility to persons with disabilities. They provide translation capabilities for clients who have a different primary language, when feasible. Counselors acknowledge the imperfect nature of such translations and accessibilities.

H.6. Social Media

H.6.a. Virtual Professional Presence

In cases where counselors wish to maintain a professional and personal presence for social media use, separate professional and personal web pages and profiles are created to clearly distinguish between the two kinds of virtual presence.

H.6.b. Social Media as Part of Informed Consent

Counselors clearly explain to their clients, as part of the informed consent procedure, the benefits, limitations, and boundaries of the use of social media.

H.6.c. Client Virtual Presence

Counselors respect the privacy of their clients' presence on social media unless given consent to view such information.

H.6.d. Use of Public Social Media

Counselors take precautions to avoid disclosing confidential information through public social media.

Section I

Resolving Ethical Issues

Introduction

Professional counselors behave in an ethical and legal manner. They are aware that client welfare and trust in the profession depend on a high level of professional conduct. They hold other counselors to the same standards and are willing to take appropriate action to ensure that standards are upheld. Counselors strive to resolve ethical dilemmas with direct and open communication among all parties involved and seek consultation with colleagues and supervisors when necessary. Counselors incorporate ethical practice into their daily professional work and engage in ongoing professional development regarding current topics in ethical and legal issues in counseling. Counselors become familiar with the ACA Policy and Procedures for Processing Com- plaints of Ethical Violations[1] and use it as a reference for assisting in the enforcement of the *ACA Code of Ethics*.

I.1. Standards and the Law

I.1.a. Knowledge

Counselors know and understand the *ACA Code of Ethics* and other applicable ethics codes from professional organizations or certification and licensure bodies of which they are members. Lack of knowledge or misunderstanding of an ethical responsibility is not a defense against a charge of unethical conduct.

I.1.b. Ethical Decision Making

When counselors are faced with an ethical dilemma, they use and document, as appropriate, an ethical decision- making model that may include, but is not limited to, consultation; consideration of relevant ethical standards, principles, and laws; generation of potential courses of action; deliberation of risks and benefits and selection of an objective decision based on the circumstances and welfare of all involved.

I.1.c. Conflicts Between Ethics and Laws

If ethical responsibilities conflict with the law, regulations, and/or other governing legal authority, counselors make known their commitment to the *ACA Code of Ethics* and take steps to resolve the conflict. If the conflict cannot be re- solved using this approach, counselors, acting in the best interest of the client, may adhere to the requirements of the law, regulations, and/or other governing legal authority.

I.2. Suspected Violations

I.2.a. Informal Resolution

When counselors have reason to believe that another counselor is violating or has violated an ethical standard and substantial harm has not occurred, they attempt to fi resolve the issue informally with the other counselor if feasible, provided such action does not violate confidentiality rights that may be involved.

I.2.b. Reporting Ethical Violations

If an apparent violation has substantially harmed or is likely to substantially harm a person or organization and is not appropriate for informal resolution or is not resolved properly, counselors take further action depending on the situation. Such action may include referral to state or national committees on professional ethics, voluntary national certification bodies, state licensing boards, or appropriate institutional authorities. The confidentiality rights of clients should be considered in all actions. This standard does not apply when counselors have been retained to review the work of another counselor whose professional conduct is in question (e.g., consultation, expert testimony).

I.2.c. Consultation

When uncertain about whether a particular situation or course of action may be in violation of the *ACA Code of Ethics*, counselors consult with other counselors who are knowledgeable about ethics and the *ACA Code of Ethics*, with colleagues, or with appropriate authorities, such as the ACA Ethics and Professional Standards Department.

I.2.d. Organizational Conflicts

If the demands of an organization with which counselors are affiliated pose a conflict with the *ACA Code of Ethics*, counselors specify the nature of such conflicts and express to their supervisors or other responsible officials their commitment to the *ACA Code of Ethics* and, when possible, work through the appropriate channels to address the situation.

I.2.e. Unwarranted Complaints

Counselors do not initiate, participate in, or encourage the fidelity of ethics com- plaints that are retaliatory in nature or are made with reckless disregard or willful ignorance of facts that would disprove the allegation.

I.2.f. Unfair Discrimination Against Complainants and Respondents

Counselors do not deny individuals employment, advancement, admission to academic or other programs, tenure, or promotion based solely on their having made or their being the subject of an ethics complaint. This does not preclude taking action based on the outcome of such proceedings or considering other appropriate information.

I.3. Cooperation With Ethics Committees

Counselors assist in the process of enforcing the *ACA Code of Ethics*. Counselors cooperate with investigations, proceedings, and requirements of the ACA Ethics Committee or ethics committees of other duly constituted associations or boards having jurisdiction over those charged with a violation

Glossary of Terms

Abandonment – the inappropriate ending or arbitrary termination of a counseling relationship that puts the client at risk.

Advocacy – promotion of the well-being of individuals, groups, and the counseling profession within systems and organizations. Advocacy seeks to remove barriers and obstacles that inhibit access, growth, and development.

Assent – to demonstrate agreement when a person is otherwise not capable or competent to give formal consent (e.g., informed consent) to a counseling service or plan.

Assessment – the process of collecting in-depth information about a person in order to develop a comprehensive plan that will guide the collaborative counseling and service provision process.

Bartering – accepting goods or services from clients in ex- change for counseling services.

Client – an individual seeking or referred to the professional services of a counselor.

Confidentiality – the ethical duty of counselors to protect a client's identity, identifying characteristics, and private communications.

Consultation – a professional relationship that may include, but is not limited to, seeking advice, information, and/ or testimony.

Counseling – a professional relationship that empowers diverse individuals, families, and groups to accomplish mental health, wellness, education, and career goals.

Counselor Educator – a professional counselor engaged primarily in developing, implementing, and supervising the educational preparation of professional counselors.

Counselor Supervisor – a professional counselor who engages in a formal relationship with a practicing counselor or counselor-in-training for the purpose of overseeing that individual's counseling work or clinical skill development.

Culture – membership in a socially constructed way of living, which incorporates collective values, beliefs, norms, boundaries, and lifestyles that are co-created with others who share similar worldviews comprising biological, psychosocial, historical, psychological, and other factors.

Discrimination – the prejudicial treatment of an individual or group based on their actual or perceived membership in a particular group, class, or category.

Distance Counseling – The provision of counseling services by means other than face-to-face meetings, usually with the aid of technology.

Diversity – the similarities and differences that occur within and across cultures, and the intersection of cultural and social identities.

Documents – any written, digital, audio, visual, or artistic recording of the work within the counseling relationship between counselor and client.

Encryption – process of encoding information in such a way that limits access to authorized users.

Examinee – a recipient of any professional counseling service that includes educational, psychological, and career appraisal, using qualitative or quantitative techniques.

Exploitation – actions and/or behaviors that take advantage of another for one's own benefit or gain.

Fee Splitting – the payment or acceptance of fees for client referrals (e.g., percentage of fee paid for rent, referral fees).

Forensic Evaluation – the process of forming professional opinions for court or other legal proceedings, based on professional knowledge and expertise, and supported by appropriate data.

Gatekeeping – the initial and ongoing academic, skill, and dispositional assessment of students' competency for professional practice, including remediation and termination as appropriate.

Impairment – a significantly diminished capacity to perform professional functions.

Incapacitation – an inability to perform professional functions.

Informed Consent – a process of information sharing associated with possible actions clients may choose to take, aimed at assisting clients in acquiring a full appreciation and understanding of the facts and implications of a given action or actions.

Instrument – a tool, developed using accepted research practices, that measures the presence and strength of a specified construct or constructs.

Interdisciplinary Teams – teams of professionals serving clients that may include individuals who may not share counselors' responsibilities regarding confidentiality.

Minors – generally, persons under the age of 18 years, un- less otherwise designated by statute or regulation. In some jurisdictions, minors may have the right to consent to counseling without consent of the parent or guardian.

Multicultural/Diversity Competence – counselors' cultural and diversity awareness and knowledge about self and others, and how this awareness and knowledge are applied effectively in practice with clients and client groups.

Multicultural/Diversity Counseling – counseling that recognizes diversity and embraces approaches that support the worth, dignity, potential, and uniqueness of individuals within their historical, cultural, economic, political, and psychosocial contexts.

Personal Virtual Relationship – engaging in a relationship via technology and/or social media that blurs the professional boundary (e.g., friending on social networking sites); using personal accounts as the connection point for the virtual relationship.

Privacy – the right of an individual to keep oneself and one's personal information free from unauthorized disclosure.

Privilege – a legal term denoting the protection of confidential information in a legal proceeding (e.g., subpoena, deposition, testimony).

Pro bono publico – contributing to society by devoting a portion of professional activities for little or no financial return (e.g., speaking to groups, sharing professional information, offering reduced fees).

Professional Virtual Relationship – using technology and/ or social media in a professional manner and maintaining appropriate professional boundaries; using business accounts that cannot be linked back to personal accounts as the connection point for the virtual relationship (e.g., a business page versus a personal profile).

Records – all information or documents, in any medium, that the counselor keeps about the client, excluding personal and psychotherapy notes.

Records of an Artistic Nature – products created by the client as part of the counseling process.

Records Custodian – a professional colleague who agrees to serve as the caretaker of client records for another mental health professional.

Self-Growth – a process of self-examination and challenging of a counselor's assumptions to enhance professional effectiveness.

Serious and Foreseeable – when a reasonable counselor can anticipate significant and harmful possible consequences.

Sexual Harassment – sexual solicitation, physical advances, or verbal/nonverbal conduct that is sexual in nature; occurs in connection with professional activities or roles; is unwelcome, offensive, or creates a hostile workplace or learning environment; and/or is sufficient severe or intense to be perceived as harassment by a reason- able person.

Social Justice – the promotion of equity for all people and groups for the purpose of ending oppression and injustice affecting clients, students, counselors, families, communities, schools, workplaces, governments, and other social and institutional systems.

Social Media – technology-based forms of communication of ideas, beliefs, personal histories, etc. (e.g., social networking sites, blogs).

Student – an individual engaged in formal graduate-level counselor education.

Supervisee – a professional counselor or counselor-in-training whose counseling work or clinical skill development is being overseen in a formal supervisory relationship by a qualified trained professional.

Supervision – a process in which one individual, usually a senior member of a given profession designated as the supervisor, engages in a collaborative relationship with another individual or group, usually a junior member(s) of a given profession designated as the supervisee(s) in order to (a) promote the growth and development of the supervisee(s), (b) protect the welfare of the clients seen by the supervisee(s), and (c) evaluate the performance of the supervisee(s).

Supervisor – counselors who are trained to oversee the professional clinical work of counselors and counselors-in-training.

Teaching – all activities engaged in as part of a formal educational program that is designed to lead to a graduate degree in counseling.

Training – the instruction and practice of skills related to the counseling profession. Training contributes to the ongoing profits of students and professional counselors.

Virtual Relationship – a non–face-to-face relationship (e.g., through social media).

Index

ACA Code of Ethics Preamble 84

ACA Code of Ethics Purpose 84

Section A: The Counseling Relationship

Section A: Introduction 86

A.1. Client Welfare 86
A.1.a. Primary Responsibility 86
A.1.b. Records and Documentation 86
A.1.c. Counseling Plans 86
A.1.d. Support Network Involvement 86
A.2. Informed Consent in the Counseling Relationship 86
A.2.a. Informed Consent 86
A.2.b. Types of Information Needed 86
A.2.c. Developmental and Cultural Sensitivity 86
A.2.d. Inability to Give Consent 86
A.2.e. Mandated Clients 87
A.3. Clients Served by Others 87
A.4. Avoiding Harm and Imposing Values 87
A.4.a. Avoiding Harm 87
A.4.b. Personal Values 87
A.5. Prohibited Noncounseling Roles and Relationships 87
A.5.a. Sexual and/or Romantic Relationships Prohibited 87
A.5.b. Previous Sexual and/or Romantic Relationships 87
A.5.c. Sexual and/or Romantic Relationships With Former Clients 87
A.5.d. Friends or Family Members 87
A.5.e. Personal Virtual Relationships With Current Clients 87
A.6. Managing and Maintaining Boundaries and Professional Relationships 87

A.6.a. Previous Relationships 87
A.6.b. Extending Counseling Boundaries 87
A.6.c. Documenting Boundary Extensions 88
A.6.d. Role Changes in the Professional Relationship 88
A.6.e. Nonprofessional Interactions or Relationships (Other Than Sexual or Romantic Interactions or Relationships) 88
A.7. Roles and Relationships at Individual, Group, Institutional, and Societal Levels 88
A.7.a. Advocacy 88
A.7.b. Confidentiality and Advocacy 88

A.8. Multiple Clients 88
A.9. Group Work 88
A.9.a. Screening 88
A.9.b. Protecting Clients 88
A.10. Fees and Business Practices 88
A.10.a. Self-Referral 88
A.10.b. Unacceptable Business Practices 88
A.10.c. Establishing Fees 88
A.10.d. Nonpayment of Fees 88
A.10.e. Bartering 89
A.10.f. Receiving Gifts 89
A.11. Termination and Referral 89
A.11.a. a. Competence Within Termination and Referral 89
A.11.b. Values Within Termination and Referral 89
A.11.c. Appropriate Termination 89
A.11.d. Appropriate Transfer of Services 89
A.12. Abandonment and Client Neglect 89

Section B: Confidentiality and Privacy

Section B: Introductions 89
B.1. Respecting Client Rights 89
B.1.a. Multicultural/Diversity Considerations 89
B.1.b. Respect for Privacy 89
B.1.c. Respect for Confidentiality 90
B.1.d. Explanation of Limitations 90
B.2. Exceptions 90
B.2.a. Serious and Foreseeable Harm and Legal Requirements 90
B.2.b. Confidentiality Regarding End-of-Life Decisions 90
B.2.c. Contagious, Life-Threatening Diseases 90
B.2.d. Court-Ordered Disclosure 90
B.2.e. Minimal Disclosure 90
B.3. Information Shared With Others 90
B.3.a. Subordinates 90
B.3.b. Interdisciplinary Teams 90
B.3.c. Confidential Settings 90
B.3.d. Third-Party Payers 90
B.3.e. Transmitting Confidential Information 90
B.3.f. Deceased Clients 90
B.4. Groups and Families 90
B.4.a. Group Work 90
B.4.b. Couples and Family Counseling 90
B.5. Clients Lacking Capacity to Give Informed Consent 90
B.5.a. Responsibility to Clients 90
B.5.b. Responsibility to Parents and Legal Guardians 90

B.5.c. Release of Confidential Information 91
B.6. Records and Documentation 91
B.6.a. Creating and Maintaining Records and Documentation 91
B.6.b. Confidentiality of Records and Documentation 91
B.6.c. Permission to Record 91
B.6.d. Permission to Observe 91
B.6.e. Client Access 91
B.6.f. Assistance With Records 91
B.6.g. Disclosure or Transfer 91
B.6.h. Storage and Disposal After Termination 91
B.6.i. Reasonable Precautions 91
B.7. Case Consultation 91
B.7.a. Respect for Privacy 91
B.7.b. Disclosure of Confidential Information 91

Section C: Professional Responsibility

Section C: Introduction 91
C.1. Knowledge of and Compliance With Standards 91
C.2. Professional Competence 91
C.2.a. Boundaries of Competence 91
C.2.b. New Specialty Areas of Practice 91
C.2.c. Qualified for Employment 91
C.2.d. Monitor Effectiveness 91
C.2.e. Consultations on Ethical Obligations 91
C.2.f. Continuing Education 92
C.2.g. Impairment 92
C.2.h. Counselor Incapacitation, Death, Retirement, or Termination of Practice 92
C.3. Advertising and Soliciting Clients 92
C.3.a. Accurate Advertising 92
C.3.b. Testimonials 92
C.3.c. Statements by Others 92
C.3.d. Recruiting Through Employment 92
C.3.e. Products and Training Advertisements 92
C.3.f. Promoting to Those Served 92
C.4. Professional Qualifications 92
C.4.a. Accurate Representation 92
C.4.b. Credentials 92
C.4.c. Educational Degrees 92
C.4.d. Implying Doctoral-Level Competence 92
C.4.e. Accreditation Status 92
C.4.f. Professional Membership 92
C.5. Nondiscrimination 92
C.6. Public Responsibility 93
C.6.a. Sexual Harassment 93
C.6.b. Reports to Third Parties 93
C.6.c. Media Presentations 93
C.6.d. Exploitation of Others 93
C.6.e. Contributing to the Public Good (*Pro Bono Publico*) 93
C.7. Treatment Modalities 93
C.7.a. Scientific Basis for Treatment 93
C.7.b. Development and Innovation 93
C.7.c. Harmful Practices 93
C.8. Responsibility to Other Professionals 93
C.8.a. Personal Public Statements 93

Section D: Relationships With Other Professionals

Section D: Introduction 93
D.1. Relationships With Colleagues, Employers, and Employees 93
D.1.a. Different Approaches 93
D.1.b. Forming Relationships 93
D.1.c. Interdisciplinary Teamwork 93
D.1.d. Establishing Professional and Ethical

Obligations..................................94
D.1.e. Confidentiality.............................94

D.1.f. Personnel Selection and Assignment...94
D.1.g. Employer Policies........................94
D.1.h. Negative Conditions......................94
D.1.i. Protection From Punitive Action........94
D.2. Provision of Consultation Services.......94
D.2.a. Consultant Competency...................94
D.2.b. Informed Consent in Formal
Consultation................................94

Section E: Evaluation, Assessment, and Interpretation

Section E: Introduction.............................94

E.1. General......................................94
E.1.a. Assessment 94
E.1.b. Client Welfare............................94
E.2. Competence to Use and Interpret
Assessment Instruments......................94
E.2.a. Limits of Competence...................
E.2.b. Appropriate Use..........................95
E.2.c. Decisions Based on Results...............95
E.3. Informed Consent in Assessment.........95
E.3.a. Explanation to Clients....................95
E.3.b. Recipients of Results.....................95
E.4. Release of Data to Qualified
Personnel....................................95
E.5. Diagnosis of Mental Disorders.............95
E.5.a. Proper Diagnosis..........................95
E.5.b. Cultural Sensitivity.......................95
E.5.c. Historical and Social Prejudices in the
Diagnosis of Pathology....................95
E.5.d. Refraining From
Diagnosis...................................95
E.6. Instrument Selection.........................95
E.6.a. Appropriateness of
Instruments..................................95
E.6.b. Referral Information......................95
E.7. Conditions of Assessment Administration
E.7.a. Administration
Conditions..................................95
E.7.b. Provision of Favorable Conditions.....95
E.7.c. Technological Administration............95
E.7.d. Unsupervised
Assessments.................................95
E.8. Multicultural Issues/Diversity in
Assessment...................................96
E.9. Scoring and Interpretation of
Assessments..................................96
E.9.a. Reporting..................................96
E.9.b. Instruments With Insufficient Empirical
Data..96
E.9.c. Assessment Services......................96
E.10. Assessment Security........................96
E.11. 1. Obsolete Assessment and Outdated
Results.......................................96
E.12. Assessment Construction..................96
E.13. Forensic Evaluation: Evaluation for
Legal Proceedings..........................96
E.13.a. Primary Obligations.....................96
E.13.b. Consent for Evaluation..................96
E.13.c. Client Evaluation
Prohibited.................................96
E.13.d. Avoid Potentially Harmful
Relationships.............................96

Section F: Supervision, Training, and Teaching

Section F: Introduction...........................97

F.1. Counselor Supervision and Client
Welfare......................................97
F.1.a. Client Welfare.............................97
F.1.b. Counselor Credentials....................97
F.1.c. Informed Consent and Client Rights...97
F.2. Counselor Supervision Competence   97
F.2.a. Supervisor Preparation...................97

F.2.b. Multicultural Issues/Diversity in
Supervision................................97
F.2.c. Online Supervision........................97
F.3. Supervisory Relationship...................97
F.3.a. Extending Conventional Supervisory
Relationships...............................97
F.3.b. Sexual Relationships.....................97
F.3.c. Sexual Harassment........................97
F.3.d. Friends or Family Members..............97
F.4. Supervisor Responsibilities.................97
F.4.a. Informed Consent for Supervision......97
F.4.b. Emergencies and Absences..............97
F.4.c. Standards for Supervisees................97
F.4.d. Termination of the Supervisory
Relationship..............................97
F.5. Student and Supervisee
Responsibilities.............................99
F.5.a. Ethical Responsibilities..................99
F.5.b. Impairment................................99
F.5.c. Professional Disclosure..................99
F.6. Counseling Supervision Evaluation,
Remediation, and Endorsement..........99
F.6.a. Evaluation.................................99
F.6.b. Gatekeeping and Remediation.........99
F.6.c. Counseling for Supervisees..............99
F.6.d. Endorsements.............................99
F.7. Responsibilities of Counselor
Educators....................................98
F.7.a. Counselor Educators....................98
F.7.b. Counselor Educator Competence....98
F.7.c. Infusing Multicultural Issues
/Diversity.................................98
F.7.d. Integration of Study and Practice........98
F.7.e. Teaching Ethics..........................98
F.7.f. Use of Case Examples...................99
F.7.g. Student-to-Student Supervision and
Instruction................................99
F.7.h. Innovative Theories and Techniques..99
F.7.i. Field Placements 99
F.8. Student Welfare 99
F.8.a. Program Information and Orientation
....99
F.8.b. Student Career Advising 99
F.8.c. Self-Growth Experiences 99
F.8.d. Addressing Personal Concerns.........99
F.9. Evaluation and Remediation..............99
F.9.a. Evaluation of Students 99
F.9.b. Limitations 99
F.9.c. Counseling for Students 99
F.10. Roles and Relationships Between
Counselor Educators and Students 100
F.10.a. Sexual or Romantic Relationships...100
F.10.b. Sexual Harassment.....................100
F.10.c. Relationships With Former
Students...................................100
F.10.d. Nonacademic Relationships..........100
F.10.e. Counseling Services....................100
F.10.f. Extending Educator–Student
Boundaries................................100
F.11. in Counselor Education and Training
Programs....................................100
F.11.a. .a. Faculty Diversity....................100
F.11.b. .b. Student Diversity....................100
F.11.c. .c. Multicultural/Diversity and
Competence................................100

Section G: Research and Publication ....

Section G: Introduction..........................100

G.1.a. Research Responsibilities 100

G.1.b. Conducting Research.....................100
G.1.c. Confidentiality in Research.............100
G.1.d. Independent Researchers................101
G.1.e. Deviation From Standard Practice......101
G.1.f. Precautions to Avoid Injury.............101
G.1.g.Principal Researcher Responsibility....101
G.2. Rights of Research Participants..........101
G.2.a. Informed Consent in Research.........101
G.2.b. Student/Supervisee Participation.......101
G.2.c. Client Participation......................101
G.2.d. Confidentiality of Information.........101
G.2.e. Persons Not Capable of Giving Informed
Consent....................................101
G.2.f. Commitments to Participants............101
G.2.g. Explanations After Data Collection....101
G.2.h. Informing Sponsors......................101
G.2.i. Research Records
Custodian..................................101
G.3. Managing and Maintaining
Boundaries..................................101
G.3.a. Extending Researcher–Participant
Boundaries...............................101
G.3.b. Relationships With Research Participants
....102
G.3.c. Sexual Harassment and Research
Participants...............................102
G.4. Reporting Results...........................102
G.4.a. Accurate Results.........................102
G.4.b. Obligation to Report Unfavorable
Results....................................102
G.4.c. Reporting Errors.........................102

G.4.d. Identity of Participants..................102
G.4.e. Replication Studies......................102
G.5. Publications and Presentations............102
G.5.a. Use of Case Examples...................102
G.5.b. Plagiarism................................102
G.5.c. Acknowledging Previous Work.........102
G.5.d. Contributors.............................102
G.5.e. Agreement of Contributors..............102
G.5.f. Student Research........................102
G.5.g. Duplicate Submissions..................102
G.5.h. Professional Review.....................102

Section H: Distance Counseling, Technology, and Social Media

Section H: Introduction..........................103

H.1. Knowledge and Legal Considerations   103
H.1.a. Knowledge and Competency...........103
H.1.b. Laws and Statutes.......................103
H.2. Informed Consent and Security..........103
H.2.a. Informed Consent and Disclosure.....103
H.2.b. Confidentiality Maintained by the
Counselor   103
H.2.c. Acknowledgment of Limitations.......103
H.2.d. Security...................................103
H.3. Client Verification.........................103
H.4. Distance Counseling Relationship.......103
H.4.a. Benefits and Limitations................103
H.4.b. Professional Boundaries in Distance
Counseling...............................103
H.4.c. Technology-Assisted Services..........104
H.4.d. Effectiveness of Services...............104

H.4.e. Access......................................104
H.4.f. Communication Differences in Electronic
Media..104
H.5. Records and Web Maintenance...........104
H.5.a. Records....................................104
H.5.b. Client Rights.............................104
H.5.c. Electronic Links.........................104
H.5.d. Multicultural and Disability
Considerations............................104

H.6. Social Media..............................104
  H.6.a. Virtual Professional Presence.........104
  H.6.b. Social Media as Part of Informed Consent................................104
  H.6.c. Client Virtual Presence.................104
  H.6.d. Use of Public Social Media..................................104

Section I: Resolving Ethical Issues ....

Section I: Introduction 104

I.1. Standards and the Law....................105
  I.1.a. Knowledge...............................105
  I.1.b. Ethical Decision Making...................................105
  I.1.c. Conflicts Between Ethics and Laws 105
I.2. Suspected Violations........................105
  I.2.a. Informal Resolution.....................105
  I.2.b. Reporting Ethical Violations.............................105
  I.2.c. Consultation..............................105
  I.2.d. Organizational Conflicts................................105
  I.2.e. Unwarranted Complaint................105
  I.2.f. Unfair Discrimination Against Complainants and Respondents...............................105
I.3. Cooperation With Ethics Committees...............................105

Glossary of Terms..............................106

Ethics Related Resources From ACA!

- Free consultation on ethics for ACA Members
- Bestselling publications revised in accordance with the 2014 *Code of Ethics*, including *ACA Ethical Standards Casebook*, *Boundary Issues in Counseling*, *Ethics Desk Reference for Counselors*, and *The Counselor and the Law*
- Podcast and six-part webinar series on the 2014 *Code*
- The latest information on ethics at *counseling.org/ethics*

AMERICAN COUNSELING ASSOCIATION

5999 Stevenson Avenue

Alexandria, VA 22304

counseling.org • 800-422-2648 x222

Note: This document may be reproduced in its entirety without permission for non-commercial purposes only.

Note: The American Counseling Association. Reprinted with permission. No further reproduction authorized without written permission from the American Counseling Association.

REFERENCES

American Counseling Association (2014). Code of Ethics. Alexandria, VA: Author.

Corey, G., Corey, M., & Callanan, M. (2015). *Issues and Ethics in the Helping Professions, 9th Edition.* Pacific Grove, CA: Brooks/Cole.

Forester-Miller, H. & Davis, T. (2016) Practitioner's Guide to Ethical Decision Making. American Counseling Association. Alexandria, VA.

Forester-Miller, H. & Davis, T. (1996) A Practitioner's Guide to Ethical Decision Making. American Counseling Association. Alexandria, VA.

Herlihy, B. & Corey, G. (2015). *ACA Ethical Standards Casebook, 7th ed.* Alexandria, VA: ACA Distribution.

Sheperis, D. & Sheperis, C. (2015). *Clinical Mental Health Counseling: Fundamentals of Applied Practice.* Upper Saddle River, NJ: Pearson.

www.ingramcontent.com/pod-product-compliance
Lightning Source LLC
Chambersburg PA
CBHW080523030426
42337CB00023B/4609